CANEWORK

CANEWORK

Kay Johnson

DRYAD PRESS LTD LONDON

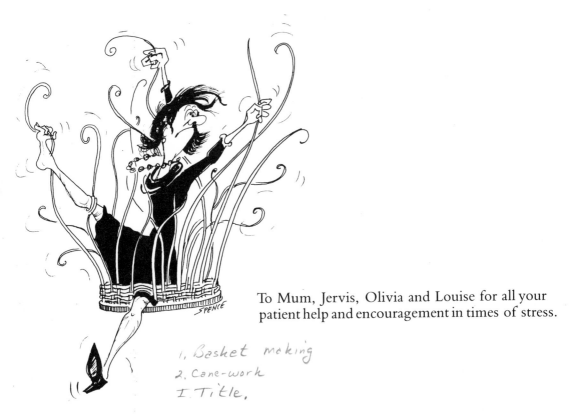

To Mum, Jervis, Olivia and Louise for all your
patient help and encouragement in times of stress.

1, Basket making
2. Cane-work
I. Title,

First published 1986

ISBN 0 8521 9606 7

Typeset by Chelmsford Origination Limited,
Chelmsford, Essex and printed in Great Britain by
Anchor Brendon Limited, Tiptree, Essex for the
publishers Dryad Press Ltd. 4 Fitzhardinge Street
London W1H 0AH

Contents

0870

Acknowledgment

I am particularly indebted to:

Susan Colman for her help with the graphics
Bill and Felicity Crawforth for the drawings
Daphne Davies for typing the manuscript
Barbara Larcom for her help with the
photographs
Rev. Philip Spence for the cartoon
Nellie Pilcher for showing me her method of
working a square cane basket

I would like to thank members of the Basketmakers' Association for all the letters and ques-
tionnaires they answered so fully, and the many
other friends who have helped and encouraged
me.

Dryad kindly supplied all the material used
in the baskets illustrated.

Introduction

I have written this book with the complete beginner in mind. The text describes in detail the techniques and basketry terminology used and there are over eighty diagrams and photographs to help you.

Each chapter uses the skills learned in the previous one, so it is *very important to start at Chapter 1* and work systematically through.

Cane, imported from the Far East, is relatively inexpensive and can be purchased at most craft shops. It comes in about fifteen different sizes but, in order to make things as simple as possible, I have kept the number down to a minimum. The materials and tools needed are clearly listed for each project.

Each chapter teaches you how to make an attractive and useful basket. By following the simple instructions for colouring cane, and then including it with the natural material, interest and a unique touch can be added to each creation.

The first basket is made on a wooden base so the beginner can concentrate on learning the basic weaves. The second chapter gives instruction on how to weave a table mat; this is basically the same technique as a woven basket base. Subsequently each basket has instructions for making with both a wooden and a woven base, so that the reader can choose which ever method is preferred.

Experimentation is great fun and basketry is a very satisfying craft. I do hope that after working your way through this book you will have had many hours of enjoyment, either on your own or in a class and that you will have gained a sound knowledge of basketry and its traditional vocabulary.

Materials and their preparation

You can buy several different qualities of cane or, more correctly, centre cane (so called because it is made from the centre or pulp of the rattan plant). I would recommend using the natural superior quality. Some of the cheaper varieties are brittle and ragged and consequently far less pleasant to work with. It is very difficult to make good baskets from poor material.

Cane is usually sold in ¼ kg hanks and comes in all sizes from 1 mm to 12 mm (Fig. 1).

Fig 1 *Cane sizes*

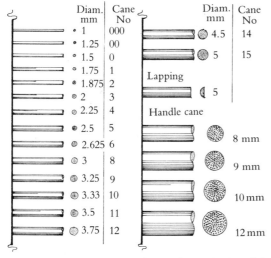

Diam. mm	Cane No
• 1	000
• 1.25	00
∘ 1.5	0
∘ 1.75	1
• 1.875	2
∘ 2	3
∘ 2.25	4
◉ 2.5	5
◎ 2.625	6
◉ 3	8
◉ 3.25	9
◉ 3.33	10
◉ 3.5	11
◉ 3.75	12

Diam. mm	Cane No
◉ 4.5	14
◉ 5	15
Lapping	
◖ 5	
Handle cane	
◉	8 mm
◉	9 mm
◉	10 mm
◉	12 mm

In this book I have only used nos 3, 6 and 8 in the first few chapters, nos 10–15 are used later on.

Bleached cane is available. This is very much softer to work with so may be more suitable in some remedial classes. It dyes well and is particularly good for light colours. It also turns sharp corners well without cracking or kinking.

Smoked cane, a nice chocolate brown colour, is available from some suppliers.

Rotacane is a synthetic imitation of centre cane. It is useful in some therapy classes as it comes in a continuous coil and requires no soaking. The finished work does not compare, however, with good quality centre cane.

Many different materials can be introduced into the weaving to give variety of colour and texture. Once you become confident, and have mastered the basic techniques of basketry, you may like to experiment, adding either seagrass, or raffia, rush, strawplait, coloured shoots from hedgerow woods, coloured plastic wrapping tape, plaited baler twine, beads threaded on the cane, even brightly coloured cereal packets cut into narrow strips and woven in to introduce colour between the rows of natural cane.

PREPARATION

The beauty of centre cane is that it needs little or no preparation beforehand. You can just pick it up and dip it in water and begin work when you get the urge!

It should not be worked dry or it may crack and you won't be able to shape your basket properly. The smaller sizes (3 and 6 in this book) usually need only a short dipping in warm water. *Never* leave the cane soaking longer than necessary as it will discolour and become rough and ragged.

Always dry thoroughly any unused cane before putting it away and *never* store your unfinished dampened basket in a plastic bag, or even carry it home from a class in one. If you forget to remove it when you get home, next time you look at it you may find the cane has developed ugly spots of black mould.

The soaking time that the different thicknesses of cane need varies from sample to sample. You will soon discover how long is required for the cane to become soft by trying the different grades in warm water.

Tools

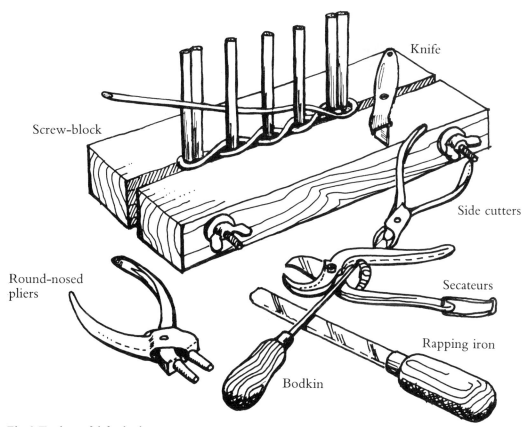

Knife

Screw-block

Side cutters

Round-nosed pliers

Secateurs

Rapping iron

Bodkin

Fig 2 Tools useful for basketry

Knife For pointing the ends of the cane and for general use.

Screw-block Not required until Chapter 11 when directions are given for its construction.

Round-nosed pliers Used for squeezing the damp cane before bending to prevent splitting when an acute angle is required.

9

Side cutters For general use throughout the making of a basket and for cutting off the surplus ends.

Tape measure or ruler

Bodkin Used for splitting base sticks and enlarging spaces in the weaving to insert handles etc. A knitting needle makes quite a good substitute.

Secateurs For cutting the larger sizes of cane.

Rapping iron Can be used (with caution) to tap down the weaving on the side of the basket to keep it even.

A weight, approximately 2 lb Placed inside the basket to steady it while the work is in progress. This can be a large stone, flat iron, etc.

1 Plant pot basket

This little basket will hold a plant pot
with a 5 cm (2 in) base. It could also
be used as a gift for a new mum, pink
or blue ribbon laced through the loops and the
basket filled with cotton wool for the baby. Or
perhaps a Mother's Day present holding a jam
jar containing a posy of flowers.

MATERIAL REQUIRED

Wooden base 7½ cm (3 in) with uneven number
of holes
No. 6 cane for stakes and waling
No. 3 cane for randing
(Weight of cane approx. 50 g (2 oz))

TOOLS REQUIRED

Side cutters
Ruler or tape measure
Bodkin or knitting needle
Bowl for water

Fig 3 *Starting foot border*

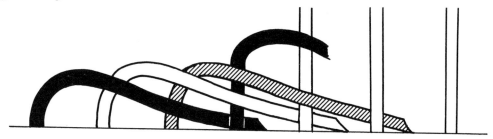

METHOD

1. Draw two or three pieces of cane from the bundle of no. 6.
2. Cut lengths 30 cm (1 ft), one for each hole in the base.
3. Soak in warm water for a minute or two until nice and pliable.

   NOTE: It is most important to have the side stakes straight. If the cane has been stored wrapped in tight bundles it may need extra soaking in warm water to straighten it out. One friend of mine recommends cutting the stakes and then tying very curved cane to a broom handle – it is then straight when it dries out.

4. Hold the base on its edge, upper side facing you, and push the damp stakes through the holes so that approximately 7½ cm (3 in) are protruding on the furthest side.
5. Bend one of these short ends over sideways, take it in front of the next two stakes and tuck it securely behind the next (Fig. 3). 'Take one in front of two and leave the end inside.'

   This little jingle was taught to the basket-making class at the London School of Occupational Therapy, where I first learned basketry from Albert Crampton. We all used to chant it: 'Take one in front of two and leave the end inside.' Twenty-eight years later it still reminds me how to do a foot border on a wooden base!

6. Continue round the base, until only three stakes are left unwoven, A, B and C.

   NOTE: At this point ease the first three stakes up a little so there is room for B and C to be tucked under.

7. Take A first, in front of B and C and tuck the end inside behind the first stake you turned down.
8. Next B, in front of C and the first turned down stake and tuck the end inside.
9. Finally C, in front of the first two, and leave the end inside tucking it under the second stake from the beginning so it rests against the third.

   PITFALL: Make sure the ends of A, B and C are all inside and lying on the wooden base, as in Fig. 4.

10. This completes the foot border. Pull all the stakes tight on the upper side and bend them slightly outwards so that the flower pot will fit comfortably inside on the base.

WALING (THE UPSETT)

This is weaving with three or more lengths of cane, worked in sequence. Three rows will be woven to 'set the stakes up' (upsett) in the right position and waling is the stroke used.

1. Damp three lengths of no. 6 cane about 1 m (3 ft) long. Not too long or it may tangle; it's easier to join than undo a messy knot of cane (Fig. 5).

Fig 4 *Finishing foot border*

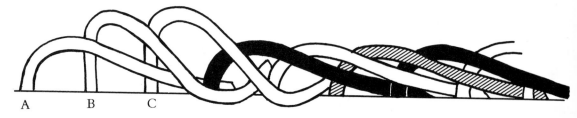

A   B   C

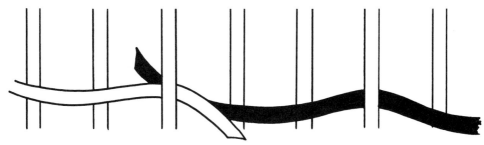

Fig 5 *Joining waling*

2. Redamp the stakes if dry and push them gently outwards. The shape of your basket must be considered right from the start. The stroke you are about to learn is going to be the foundation of your basket, holding the stakes firmly in the right position. In this case your basket will need to flow gently outwards from the base if it is going to hold a flower pot.

3. Place a weight, or a jar containing something to give it weight (jam?) on the base within the stakes. This will keep the basket firmly on the table as you work and help with the shaping. It is most important to *always* weight the inside of the basket to keep it steady, and allow you to use both hands for shaping and weaving.

4. Place a light plastic clothes peg on any one of the stakes 15 cm (6 in) up from the base. This is to act as a marker showing you where the waling started.

5. Put the three lengths of no. 6 cane (which has just been dipped in water, *not* soaked for a long time, as this will spoil the colour and texture) in three consecutive spaces, A to the right of the marked stake, B to the right of that, and then C furthest right (the short ends inside pointing to the left) (Fig. 6).

These ends shouldn't be too long, but just lie behind the stake they lean against.

6. Take A, go in front of two stakes, behind the next and out to the front.

7. Take B, go in front of two, behind one and out to the front.

8. Take C, go in front of two, behind one and out to the front. Don't pull the cane, handle it lightly. The left hand controls the shape of the basket and the right hand guides the cane in and out of the stakes.

9. Take these three canes in turn, travelling to the right round the basket. Each stroke goes in front of 'two' and behind 'one'. I find it easiest to move my left hand so my index finger is always behind the two stakes when the weaving cane is passed in front of them, and brought behind the next stake. This helps to stop the tendency for the stakes to be bent inwards. The left hand should be continually shaping the basket in this way, adjusting the stakes, seeing they remain upright, not bending to the left or the right, helping them to flow outwards when required, or to go straight upwards, etc. The left hand should also press the cane firmly down on the last row. Don't forget, you are master of the cane, and you can make it do

Fig 6 *Starting waling*

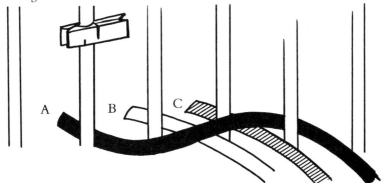

exactly what you want – with practice! Don't worry if you are left-handed, work in exactly the same direction as described. The left hand is doing most of the work anyway.

THE STEP-UP, OR 'CHANGING-THE-STROKE'

When the first cane reaches the left-hand side of the marked stake, you have three more strokes to finish your first round of waling. Here, in order to complete the round with no visible difference in the stroke, it is necessary to 'change-the-stroke', reversing the order for one stroke each (C, B, A).

SNAG: Never join in a new cane near the change-of-stroke.

1. C is taken first, in front of two and then behind one and out to the front.
2. B is taken in front of two and behind one and out to the front.
3. A is taken in front of two and then behind one and out to the front. So now you will see (Fig. 7) that

C is lying on top of the starting point of C

B is lying on top of the starting point of B and

A is lying on top of the starting point of A

and is on the right side of the marker. Your first row of waling is complete. Do not worry if the 'stroke' looks different, just check that A, B and C are on top of the three starting ends.

4. Continue the next round, taking A, then B and then C just as you did in the beginning, until you reach the left of the marked stake

again, then reverse the order to change-the-stroke (the step-up) C, then B, and then A, so again these three lie on top of the starting ends. Now continue working with A, then B, then C. Change-the-stroke each time you reach the marked stake until the end of the final row.

FINISHING WALING

1. When you have completed the required number of rows (in this case three) and reached the marked stake for the last time, take A first, in front of two and behind one and leave the end outside (Fig. 8).
2. B next in front of two, behind one, and *under* one (the previous row) bringing the end out to the front.
3. C next, in front of two, behind one and this time under *two*, bringing the end out to the front.
4. A, B and C now lie under two canes each and in between the same stakes as they did at the start. Press the upsetting down firmly with your fingers, so there are no gaps, and cut the ends off neatly on the outside. Hold the side cutters against the side of the basket, make the cut slant so that no ends can be felt when you run your hand over the basket.

BYE-STAKING

These are used to strengthen the main stakes and make a firm framework for the basket.

1. Cut thirteen bye-stakes (or the correct number to correspond with the stakes) from no. 6 cane, 10 cm (4 in) long.

Fig 7 *Changing-the-stroke (step-up) waling*

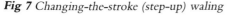

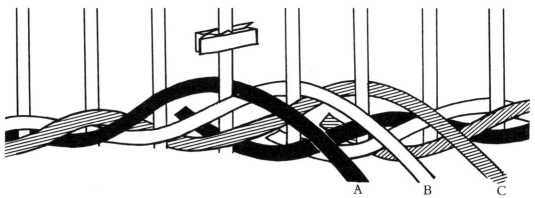

A   B   C

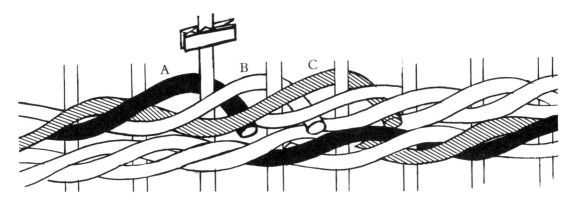

Fig 8 *Finishing waling*   **Fig 9** *Randing*

2. Insert one on the right-hand side of each stake. To make a space for the bye-stake carefully insert a bodkin, or knitting needle, next to the stake and down to the base so the weaving parts a little to allow room for the bye-stake. (It is also much easier to do this if you have removed the jam jar first!)

RANDING

This is weaving continuously with one length of cane, in this case to a depth of 6½ cm (2½ in).

1. Take a length of no. 3 cane and dip it in water. No. 3 cane is used because it is only half the size of no. 6 which was used for the stakes. You must always weave the side of your basket with a thinner size of cane than that of the stakes, otherwise your basket will be pushed out of shape by the weavers 'ruling' the stakes.
2. Replace the jam jar (making sure the top is on securely!).
3. Insert the end of the no. 3 cane inside the basket against a stake and its bye-stake.
4. Place the index finger of your left hand on the end of the cane to hold it in place and take the cane in front of the next stake and bye-stake to the right and behind the next.

   As you work, turn the basket round. Put the tip of the index finger of your left hand behind the stake you are weaving across, ease this stake out slightly, loop the cane (Fig. 9) through the gap between this and the next stake and bye-stake, hold with the left thumb, and pull the loop out to the

front with the index finger and thumb of the right hand. 'In with the thumb and out with the finger!' is the way to do it.

5. Continue to rand in and out, shaping with the left hand, making sure the stakes are parallel to each other, not being pulled inwards *too* much and keeping the shape that you want. Join a new piece of cane when necessary (Fig. 10).

   PITFALL: Trim the ends inside your basket as you go along; it may be difficult to get your hand inside to snip off any long ends when the basket is finished.
6. Continue to weave in and out until you have completed about 6½ cm (2½ in) of randing. Cut off the cane so the end lies behind the last stake.

NOW CHANGE TO WALING

This is done for two rows using the same stroke as you did at the beginning of the basket when it was known as upsetting.

Fig 10 *Joining randing*

1. Three pieces of no. 6 cane dipped into water for about a minute. Place the clothes peg as a marker on any stake you choose as your start. The first cane goes in the space to the right of the peg, the second and third in the next two consecutive spaces, as shown in Fig. 6.
2. Weave two rows of waling, remembering to change-the-stroke each time you reach the marker.

   NOTE: A band of waling should always be put on a basket just before the border; this gives strength and makes the edge much more rigid. Waling can also be added elsewhere in the siding of the basket, to give strength or simply for decoration.
3. Finish the waling as in Fig. 8. Cut the ends off neatly with side cutters. Next cut off the bye-stakes level with the top of the waling.

   PITFALL: Be very careful *not* to cut off the long stake by mistake! Pull the stake slightly to the left so that you have room to cut the bye-stake without nicking the stake itself. Press down on the waling with the side cutters, so that the bye-stake is cut as short as possible.

SIMPLE SCALLOP BORDER

1. Soak the top of the stakes for a few minutes, in hot water, until they are nice and pliable.
2. Cut the end of one stake to a point, bring it in front of the next stake to the right, and down into the weaving on the left of the next stake (Fig. 11).
3. Decide what height you want the loop to be; about 2 cm (¾ in) between the underside of the loop and the top of the basket is about right.

   SNAG: Make sure the end goes firmly down into at least seven rows of randing below the waling so that later, when the basket is dry, the stakes will not come undone.
4. If the stake is too long, pull the loop out, cut a piece off and try it again.
5. When you are satisfied that you have the right length of stake for the loop, cut all the other stakes, with a diagonal cut, to exactly the same length, so all the loops on the border will be uniform. Re-damp the stakes if necessary; they may kink if they are too dry, instead of being nicely curved. You will probably need to use a bodkin to open the space a little on the left of each stake, so the looped end fits easily beside the other, and does not have to be forced, as this may also cause it to kink.
6. Adjust all the loops to make sure they are even.

Fig 11 *Scallop border*

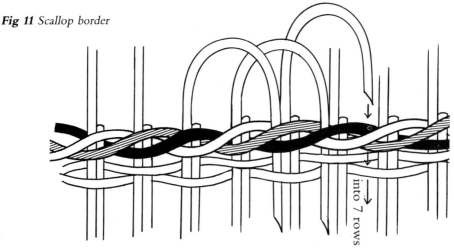

into 7 rows

2 Small and large table mats

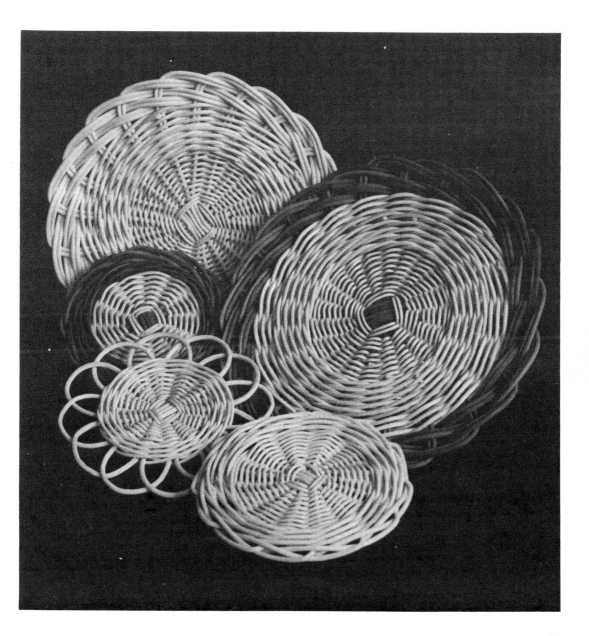

Following on from the plant pot basket, this chapter gives instructions on how to make two sizes of table mat, the first approx. 12 cm (4¾ in), the second 22 cm (8¾ in) across.

The construction of these mats is quite simple and the method almost exactly the same as for the woven base of a round basket.

When you have made one or two mats you may like to try the woven base in some of the following chapters.

The mats can be made using dyed cane for sticks, so the border is coloured (see instructions, p.39). Commercial 'smoked' cane can be used as in the illustration.

SMALL MAT

MATERIAL REQUIRED

No. 8 cane for sticks – natural, dyed or smoked
No. 6 cane for waling.

No. 3 cane for pairing
(Approximately 25 g (1 oz) altogether)

TOOLS

Same as for the plant pot basket with the addition of a wooden board and round-nosed pliers.

METHOD

1. Cut six strands of no. 8 cane, 46 cm (18 in) long.
2. Damp them and straighten out any curved sticks.
3. Mark the middle of three of the pieces.
4. Working on a wooden board, push the bodkin through the marks so that all three are threaded on the bodkin (Fig. 12).
   NOTE: Work on a board so that you do not make holes in the table or yourself.

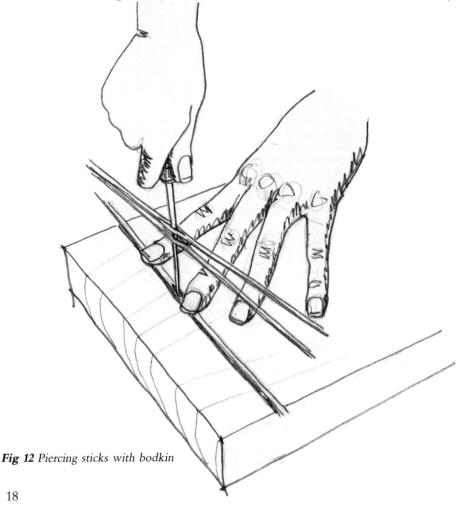

Fig 12 Piercing sticks with bodkin

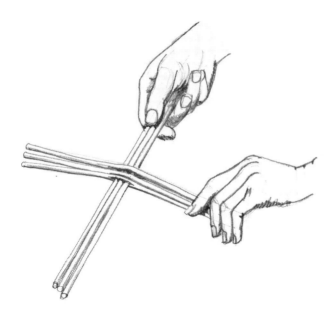

Fig 13 *The slath*

5. Now push two of the other canes through, one on either side of the bodkin, which is now removed, and the third stick pushed through in its place, so that a cross is formed, 'three through three'. This is called the slath (Fig. 13).

TYING IN THE SLATH (PAIRING)

Pairing is weaving with two canes *worked alternately* forming a twist (Fig. 14).

1. Take a length of no. 3 cane and damp it.
2. Squeeze with round nosed pliers so it won't crack when bent sharply. This should be done about one-third of the way along, so that as you work both ends will not run out together.
3. Hold the slath in your left hand, with the four groups of bottom sticks pointing north, south, east and west. Loop the no. 3 cane behind north and hold in place with your index finger (Fig. 15).
4. The left of the pair of canes 'A' is now taken firmly in front of 'north', behind 'east' and back to the front (Fig. 15).

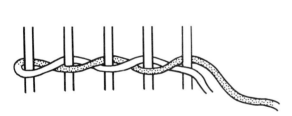

Fig 14 *Pairing*

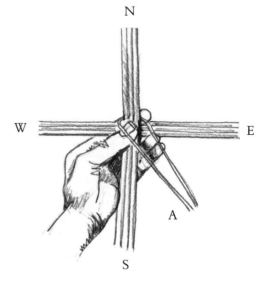

Fig 15 *Starting to tie in the slath*

N (was E)

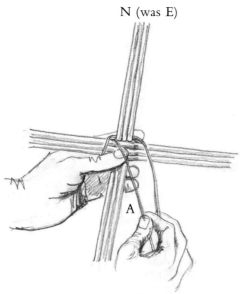

A

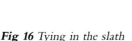

N

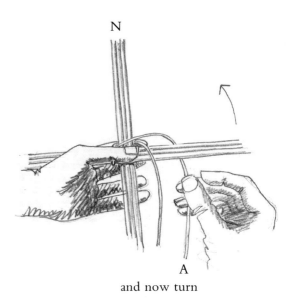

A

and now turn

Fig 16 *Tying in the slath*

5. Turn the slath a quarter turn anti-clockwise, so that 'east' becomes 'north' and the two canes which you are pairing with are in the same position as they started.
6. Take 'A' in front of 'north', behind 'east' and back to the front (Fig. 16). Turn the slath a quarter turn anti-clockwise.
7. Continue pairing round the slath in this way until each group of three sticks has two strands of pairing tying it together.

OPENING OUT THE SLATH

1. Open out the left stick of the group 'north' and bring 'B' (which was lying at the *back*) through to the front between this gap, so that both 'A' and 'B' are lying towards you (Fig.17).
2. Now take 'A' firmly to the back through the same gap.
3. Pull it tightly down on to 'B' keying it into place.
4. Open out the right-hand stick of the group and bring 'A' to the front again (and now it becomes 'B' as it is on the right of the pair).
5. Continue pairing round the slath, opening out the sticks into singles. Each time, before taking 'A' (the left-hand one of the pair), both 'A' and 'B' should be lying towards you.

Fig 17 *(below) Opening out the slath*

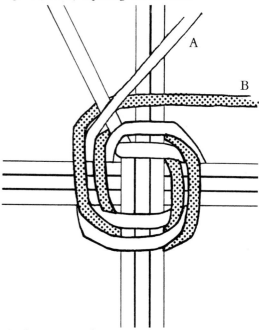

A

B

6. As you work, try to get the sticks evenly spaced, and all on the same plane (not corrugated).

SNAG: It is important to take the pairing cane *firmly* to the back and to 'key' it down on to the cane which lies below it in the space between the sticks, otherwise the rows won't lie closely on top of each other. Now bring it back gently. These are two distinct movements, first firmly to the back – pause – then gently to the front again, working alternately with the two canes and forming a twist.

JOINING

If it is necessary to join, do so when the short end is on the left of the pair, as in Fig. 18 a and b. When you have completed 6½ cm (2½ in) of pairing add a third length of no. 3 cane on the right of the two pairing weavers and begin waling.

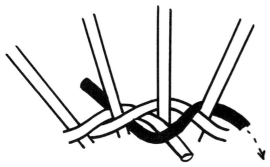

Fig 18 *(a) Joining pairing*

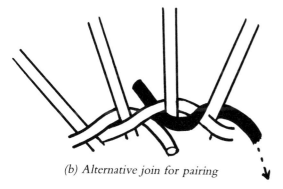

(b) Alternative join for pairing

WALING

1. Place a marker on the stake to the left of 'A' (the left-hand of the pair) as in Fig. 6 and do three rows of waling, remembering to change-the-stroke each time you reach the mark as in Fig. 7.
2. To finish off refer to Fig. 8.

SIMPLE TRAC BORDER

Border in which each stake is worked in turn, completing the movement entirely before the next stake is woven away.

SNAG: There should be at least 18 cm (7 in) of stake beyond the last row of waling in order to complete the trac border. If the stakes are too short for the simple trac use scalloped border as in last basket.

1. Soak the stakes for the border for a few minutes so the ends are really pliable.
2. Squeeze each stake with round-nosed pliers 1 cm (½ in) above the edge of the waling or else bend the stakes over half a clothes peg (Fig. 19), so all will bend at the same height and there will be room to weave away the final strokes of the border.

Fig 19 *Bending stakes for trac border*

3. Take one stake behind the next to its right, in front of the next (second), behind the next (third), in front of the next (fourth) and then tuck the end away behind the fifth (Fig. 20). So, the order is:

> behind one,
> in front of one,
> behind one,
> in front of one,
> behind one, and leave the
> end inside (at the back).

Repeat, working each stake in turn until there are four left; these must be threaded away so the pattern is continuous and the joining of the start and finish cannot be seen. HINT: If you find it difficult to weave away the last four stakes, damp the beginning of the trac border and pull out the first four stakes so they stand upright again. Now work these eight stakes in and out to match the completed part. It is easier this way to make the connection of the border perfect.

ALTERNATIVE BORDER

Instead of the simple trac border, a scallop border can be worked exactly as in Chapter 1. Suggested length of the stakes from the edge of the waling would be about 13 cm (5 in) (see Fig. 11)

Fig 20 Simple trac border

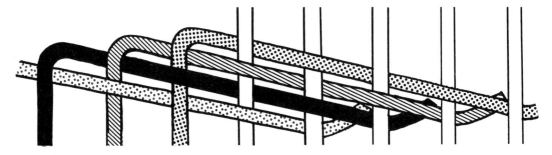

LARGE MAT

This will be approx. 22 cm (8¾ in) across.

MATERIAL REQUIRED

No. 8 cane for sticks
   and bye-stakes   } Smoked, dyed or natural
No. 6 cane for waling
No. 3 cane for pairing
(Approximately 50 g (2 oz) altogether)

METHOD

1. Damp ten strands of no. 8 cane 60 cm (24 in) long.
2. Mark the middle of five pieces, push the bodkin through so that all five are threaded on to the bodkin.
3. Check that the bodkin is exactly in the middle of the five sticks, and adjust if necessary.
4. Push one of the remaining five through beside the bodkin, remove bodkin and insert the other four sticks, so you have a slath consisting of five sticks through five.
5. Measure all the 'arms' of the slath to make sure they are equal, adjust them if necessary.

TYING IN THE SLATH

Pair round the slath twice (Figs 15 and 16) so each of the four groups of sticks have two bands of pairing across them, as in the small mat.

OPENING OUT THE SLATH

1. This time, instead of being opened out singly as in the small mat, the sticks are first divided into groups of 'two', 'one', 'two' (Fig. 21). They are paired round three times and *then* opened out singly. If you tried to open out all the sticks at once after tying in the slath, it would be difficult to get the cane firmly down between the sticks, as the

space available would be too small due to the increased number of base sticks. Groups of more than three bottom sticks are usually opened out into singles only after at least four rounds of pairing.

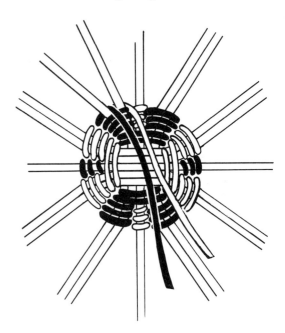

Fig 21 Opening out the slath

NOTE: An uneven number of bottom sticks (if there are more than three) should be opened out into symmetrically divided groups, as in Fig. 21. Even numbers should be divided into twos before finally being opened into singles.

2. Now open out the sticks into singles. With each pairing stroke adjust the sticks, aiming to get them all an equal distance apart and not corrugated so that the mat will lie flat when finished. As you work and the sticks

become further apart, with each stroke press the cane down firmly on to the row below, so there are no large gaps between the rows of pairing.

3. Continue pairing until you have 10 cm (4 in) across the mat. When necessary join in a new piece as in Figs 18a or b.

WALING

1. Change to no. 6 cane.
2. Take three pieces which have been dampened.
3. Place marker on one of the sticks.
4. Add three canes 'A', 'B' and 'C' in the next three consecutive spaces to the right of the marker.
   HINT: It may be difficult to hold these three canes in place at their start; a couple of clothes pegs will secure the loose ends while the first row of waling is woven.
5. Wale for four rounds. I find it easiest to place the mat flat on the table while working the wale. Remember to change-the-stroke each time the marker is reached as in Fig. 7 and finish off after four rounds of waling as in Fig. 8.
   SNAG AND PITFALL: Don't have your length of no. 6 cane too long when waling; it's easy enough to join (Fig. 5). Too long lengths may get tangled, dirty and are likely to trip up your neighbour.

PAIRING

1. Take a length of no. 6 cane.
2. Put on three rows of pairing. Keep the mat flat on the table and be careful to continue to adjust the position of the sticks to keep them all an equal distance from each other.

3. To finish off the pairing, bring the left one of the pair through to the front above the starting point and leave it there. Take the second cane to the back, round a stake and bring it to the front, tucking it under one cane in the row beneath so that both ends are held firmly.

BYE-STAKES

1. Using no. 8 cane, with a slanting cut make twenty bye-stakes 30 cm (12 in) long.
2. Using a bodkin to make room insert a bye-stake on the right beside each stick and well down into the waling.

SIMPLE TRAC BORDER

Here the bottom stick and bye-stake are taken together, so a thicker border is formed than in the smaller mat.

Make sure the cane is really pliable before you start by soaking it in hot water for a minute or two. Bend the two stakes about 2½ cm (1 in) above the edge of the waling this time, so there is room to weave away the final strokes of the border.

Now take the pairs of canes:
behind one (pair),
in front of one,
behind one,
in front of one,
behind one, and leave the end inside.
NOTE: The 'Hint' given on weaving away the last ends and making the connection of start and finish perfect applies, as in the smaller mat.

To finish, trim all ends neatly with a slanting cut and as short as possible, but make sure they are lying against a bottom stick, otherwise they may pop through to the wrong side.

3 Round cane basket with wooden base

The next two baskets are practically the same; this one is made on a wooden base and the next has a woven base. I would suggest making this one first and then going on to the woven base so that no steps are missed.

This basket (approx. 24 cm (9½ in) across top) will hold a china pâté dish which could contain a plant. Without a dish it could be used as a bread or fruit basket.

MATERIAL REQUIRED

No. 6 cane for stakes and bye-stakes
No. 6 cane for waling and chain waling
No. 3 cane for randing
Round plywood base 20 cm (8 in) diameter with twenty-nine holes
(Weight of cane approx. 50 g (2 oz))

TOOLS

As in previous chapters.

METHOD

1. Cut twenty-nine stakes from no. 6 cane, 41 cm (16 in) long, one for each hole in the base.
2. Damp in warm water and straighten out any stakes which may be curved.
3. Push the damp stakes through the holes so that approx. 7½ cm (3 in) is protruding on the side furthest from you.
4. Complete the foot border as in Figs 3 and 4, finishing carefully in sequence.
5. Gently pull each stake in turn, so that the foot border is firmly against the wooden base, and no gaps are showing.
6. Bend all the stakes slightly outwards and put the pâté dish inside so you can see how the basket must be worked, with the stakes flowing gently outwards.

WALING (UPSETTING)

1. Take three pieces of no. 6 cane long enough to go four times round the wooden base. Damp them.
2. Mark a stake with a clothes peg, bead, Sellotape or anything you have to hand which will stay in place.
3. Place the three canes in three consecutive spaces to the right of the mark and wale for three rows, remembering to change-the-stroke (Fig. 7) and to finish off correctly as in Fig. 8. As you work, bend each stake gently into an upright and slightly outward position, as all the stakes tend to bend slightly to the right when they are first worked after the foot border is completed.

BYE-STAKES

1. Using no. 6 cane, cut one bye-stake for each stake 10 cm (4 in) long.

2. Push a bye-stake in on the right side of each stake.
   PITFALL: Don't be tempted to omit the bye-stakes. No. 6 stakes by themselves will not be strong enough to keep the basket a good shape. Re-damp the stakes if they have become dry and press gently outwards.

RANDING

Using no. 3 cane, rand for approximately 2 cm (¾ in) – first placing a weight inside to keep the work steady. Bend each stake out gently with the left index finger as the weaving cane goes in front of the stake so that the basket continues its gentle outward flow.
   PITFALL: Try not to *pull* the cane as you work as this will tighten the weaving and pull the stakes inwards. Handle it lightly! Occasionally place the dish inside (if the basket is to hold one) to check that it fits.
   SNAG: Be careful if you are using anything as a weight which could leave a rust mark on the wooden base, which may be damp.
Leave the end inside when 2 cm (¾ in) of randing has been completed; this can be cut off short, but must lie against an upright stake or it will come out to the front of the basket.

CHAIN WALING

This consists of one row of waling followed by one row of reverse waling which creates the chain, used as a decorative or strengthening weave (Fig. 22). If preferred, leave out the 'chain' part of the waling and just do two rounds of waling.

Fig 22 Chain waling

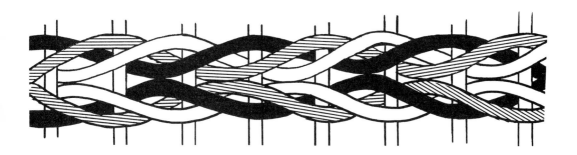

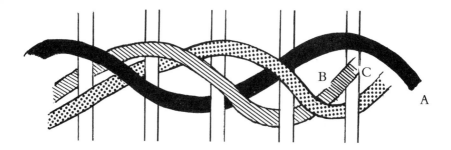

Fig 23 Reversing the stroke (after the change-of-stroke)

METHOD FOR CHAIN WALING

1. Three pieces of no. 6 cane, long enough to go three times round the basket.
2. Mark a stake and complete one round of waling, changing-the-stroke as in Fig. 7.
3. Now, instead of continuing waling as before (taking A over B and C and behind the third stake to the right) A goes *underneath* B and C and then behind the third stake to the right (Fig. 23).
4. Continue round the basket, taking A (the left-hand cane) *under* the two on its right (B and C) until the mark is reached.

FINISHING CHAIN WALING

5. Take A in front of two stakes, under B and C as before, behind one stake and leave the end *inside*.
6. Take B in front of two stakes, *under* C, thread it through under one strand of previous row and leave the end *inside*.
7. Take C in front of two stakes, thread it through under two (the previous row of

8. These ends can now be cut off neatly (or brought to the outside and used to repeat a further row of chain waling) Fig. 24)).

RANDING

Weave another 2 cm (¾ in) with no. 3 cane.

WALING

1. Mark the starting stake.
2. Take three lengths of no. 6 cane.
3. Work two rows of waling (remembering the change-of-stroke, Fit. 7), push the cane firmly down on the row below as you work, join if necessary as in Fig. 5, and finish as in Fig. 8.

TRIMMING THE BYE-STAKES

Holding each stake in turn, work round the top of the basket, pulling the stake to the left and cutting off the remaining end of the bye-stakes with side cutters.

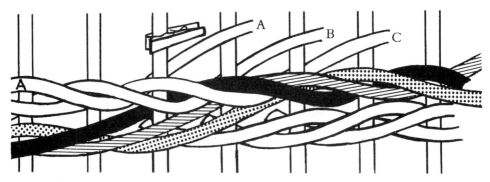

Fig 24 Showing the change-of-stroke, reverse of stroke and finish of chain waling

26

SNAG: Be very careful not to cut the stake instead of the bye-stake.

THREE ROD PLAIN BORDER

This is a strong border and is *started* by taking three rods in turn down beside their neighbour to the right (other borders may be four, five or even six rod, etc.).

1. In a basin of hot water, soak the stakes from their tips down to, and including, the top edge of the waling. They must be really pliable so there is no chance of them cracking or breaking when bent over to form the border. Five to ten minutes should be enough. Test the tip of one or two of the stakes to see if they are really soft and can be bent over at a right angle without breaking.
2. Bend each stake to the right over a pencil (or squeeze with round-nosed pliers ¾ cm (¼ in)

above the waling) so that they turn down easily for the border, and enough room is left between the top of the waling and the first three bent over stakes, to allow room for the last three to be woven away.

3. Bend one stake down behind the stake to its right and bring it out to the front. Do the same with the second and the third (Fig. 25). Now you have the three rods ready to start the three rod border.
4. Take the first rod which was bent over, in front of the stake to its right (A) behind the next (B) and out to the front (Fig. 26). Stake A is then brought down beside and *behind* it and firmly down on the top edge of the basket.
5. The second rod is now taken:
   in front of one,
   behind one,
   and the upright stake comes down beside and behind it.

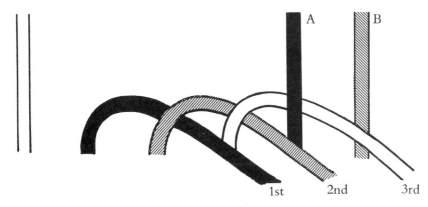

Fig 25 Starting three rod border

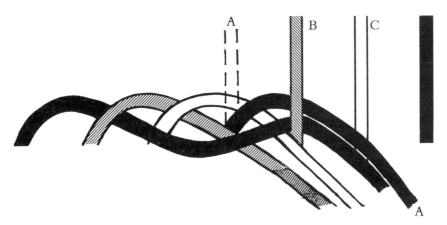

Fig 26 Continuing three rod border

6. Now the third rod in the same manner with the upright stake beside and behind it, so there are now three pairs, instead of three single rods (Fig. 27).

7. Counting from the pair of stakes furthest right, take the fifth stake (marked A) (longest of the third pair) and take it:

    in front of one,

    behind one,

    and the upright stake comes down beside and behind it.

This leaves one stake as a single (the sixth) and creates another pair furthest right. Continue round the basket taking the fifth stake each time and go in front of one, etc. as before.

8. When you have reached the first stake you turned down, and there is only one still standing, take the fifth, in front of the upright, behind the first stake marked A which was bent over, tuck it *under* this, and through to the front (Fig. 28). The upright stake comes down beside it, and is also tucked under the first bent-over stake A.

9. *Finishing the three rod border*

Take the *new* fifth stake, beside and in front of the first bent over stake A, under the next (B) and out to the front, so the *first* of the last three pairs to be woven away comes out under one stake (Fig. 29).

10. Two pairs left. Take the third alongside the next single stake to the right (B), then under C and the end of A and out to the front. (Thus the *second* to be woven away goes under *two*).

11. One pair left. Take the first alongside C

Fig 27 *Continuing three rod border*

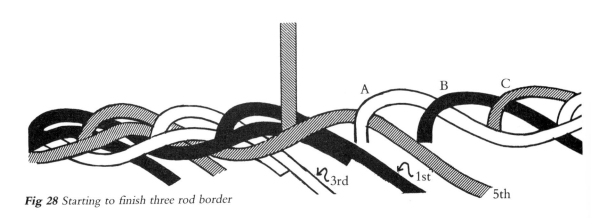

Fig 28 *Starting to finish three rod border*

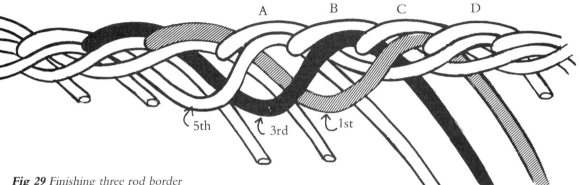

Fig 29 *Finishing three rod border*

under three (D, A and B) and out to the front. (The third to be woven away goes under three.) So, '1' goes under one,
'2' goes
    under
    two,
'3' goes
    under
    three.

Now each stake can be cut off close to the edge to finish the border or threaded through to the inside and *then* cut off, and this is called a follow-on-trac.

FOLLOW-ON-TRAC

There should be at least 8–10 cm (3-4 in) of stake left. This is used to follow the rod border to weave away the ends to the inside of the basket.

1. Shape the tip of each stake to a point. Pick up any one and, holding the basket on its side, pass this stake below the next two and, lifting the second one, push the end of the stake to the inside between the border and the waling where it will rest against the back of the next stake (Fig. 30). Continue round the basket threading each end to the inside.

2. Now the ends are cut off neatly, making sure each end is lying against a stake (Fig. 30).

PITFALL: Be very careful not to cut the ends so short that they pop through to the outside. They *must* rest against a stake on the inside of the basket.

Fig 30 *Follow-on-trac*

4 Round cane basket with woven base

This basket will be approx. 24 cm (9½ in) across the top. It is the same basket as in the last recipe, but this time the base will be woven instead of being a wooden one, so the first thing to consider is how many side stakes are needed. The wooden base had twenty-nine holes for stakes, so this one will also have *about* twenty-nine stakes.

Base sticks are the next consideration. How many? How large should the cane be? Each base stick will 'carry' four side stakes, so if you have seven base sticks you will be able to have twenty-eight side stakes.

How large should the sticks be? In order to construct a firm, strong woven base it is very important to have sturdy enough base sticks. They should always be *at least* four sizes larger than the side stakes, and even larger if you like, but never the same size, and they should never, never be smaller.

For example
1. Base sticks largest (nos 10–15).
2. Side stakes 2–4 sizes smaller than base sticks (nos 6–8).
3. Upsetting and waling smaller than side stakes (no. 6).
4. Randing and pairing smallest (no. 3).
5. Bye-stakes same as stake or smaller, though in some cases might be required to be larger.
   NOTE: Other sizes of cane are available but in this book I have used sizes 3, 6, 8 and 10–15.

MATERIAL REQUIRED

1. Base sticks will be in no. 14 cane (this was the only large size I had at the time and it made a lovely strong base, but any cane between sizes 12 and 14 is all right).
2. Side stakes will be in no. 8 cane (the last basket was done with no. 6 cane to fit the drilled holes easily).
3. Upsetting and waling will be in no. 6 cane – smaller than the side stakes.
4. Randing and pairing and bye-stakes with no. 3 cane. (Weight of cane approximately 225 g (8 oz) altogether).

TO MAKE THE BASE

The finished size should be 17½ cm (7 in).

METHOD

1. Cut seven sticks from no. 14 cane, 22 cm (8¾ in).
2. Soak in warm water for a few minutes.
3. Make a hole centrally in three sticks with a bodkin or knife. Push four sticks through the three which have been pierced to make the slath (Fig. 13 shows a slath).
   HINT: Making a slit in the cane obviously weakens it, so if you have an odd number of sticks, split the lower number, as in this case split three and push four through.

PAIRING

1. Soak a length of no. 3 cane briefly in warm water, squeeze with round nosed pliers in

the place where you want it to bend, or hold the cane with both hands close together at the point where you want it to bend in half, and twist your hands in opposite directions, so that the fibres of the cane twist. It will now bend sharply without breaking.

2. Tie in the slath (Figs 15 and 16).
3. Open out the two groups of three sticks into singles and the two groups of four sticks into doubles.
4. Pair round twice more and open out the four doubles (Fig. 21).
5. Continue opening out the sticks, remembering always to use the weaver on the left which then passes over the right weaver, spacing the sticks out evenly as you work.

CROWNING THE BASE OR WORKING THE CROWN

A woven basket base should be slightly curved, like a saucer turned upside down, so that when the basket is finished it stands firmly on the rim of the base, rather than wobbling on the pairing in the middle. The crown also gives more strength to the base.

1. As you pair round, gently but firmly shape the base sticks so they curve away from you (refer to 'Snag' following step 6, p. 20).
2. To keep the base from becoming oval rather than round, due to having an uneven number of base sticks (four through three) you will have to pull the pairing tightly away from you on to the row below between the group of three, and a little less tightly between the group of four. Continue to work like this joining where necessary (see Figs 18a and b) until the base is nicely round (and crowned!) and measures 18 cm (7 in) across.
   SNAG: Avoid joining both weavers at the same time.
3. When the base measures 18 cm (7 in) across tuck the last end under the previous row and out to the front.
4. Cut off the ends of the sticks which protrude from the edge of the base and it is now ready to be staked up.
   HINT: If the pairing on the base is a bit loose, it might be wise not to cut off the ends of the bottom sticks until you have started to

stake up, as the pairing might come off the ends of the sticks.

STAKING-UP

(Pushing side stakes into the base.)

1. Cut twenty-eight stakes 41 cm (16 in) using no. 8 cane.
2. Point the end of each one with a knife or side cutters, this is called a slype.
3. Soak about 10 cm (4 in) of the slyped end in warm water for 5–10 minutes.
4. Turn the base concave side uppermost, so it stands like a saucer *right* way up.
5. Using a bodkin (or knitting needle) to make a channel, insert the slyped end of one stake well down into the middle of the base beside one of the bottom sticks. It is very important to get the stake driven in as far as possible, otherwise it may come loose when the upsetting is started. Now insert a stake well into the pairing on the other side of the base stick. Work round the basket, inserting a stake on either side of each bottom stick (Fig. 31).

Fig 31 *Staking up the base*

NOTE: If you left the bottom sticks untrimmed because you felt the pairing might have come off at the edges, trim them now as you insert the stakes round the edge. Put in a stake and then carefully cut the end of the stick beside it. Continue in this manner, inserting *one* stake beside the stick before cutting the stick off, then insert the other stake on the other side of the trimmed stick, then on to the next.

PRICKING-UP THE STAKES

(Bending the stakes at a right angle to the base prior to starting the upsett). Willow workers would do this by pricking the rod with a knife. Cane workers squeeze the stakes with round-nosed pliers.

1. When all the stakes are firmly in place, *turn the base 'right' side up* (upside down saucer!), squeeze the damp stakes with round nosed pliers at the point where they emerge from the base, so they will bend at a right angle without breaking (Fig. 32).

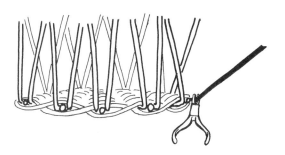

Fig 32 Pricking up the stakes

2. Secure all the ends together with string or an elastic band (the ones the postmen bring are ideal!).

THE UPSETT

This time set up the stakes first with one row of four rod wale to make a thicker rim for the basket to stand on and to hide the gap between the base and the side of the basket.

It is followed by three rows of a three rod wale, which control the ultimate shape of the basket.

1. Two full lengths of no. 6 cane, well soaked in warm water for a minute or two.
2. With the basket on its side on your lap, loop the canes round two stakes as in Fig. 33a.
3. Mark stake and work round weaving a four

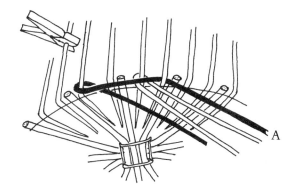

Fig 33 (a) *Starting four rod pull-down wale*

(b) *Finishing four rod, showing rod to be dropped*

rod wale – taking the left-hand rod each time, starting as in Fig. 6, but taking A in front of *three* and behind one (instead of in front of two and behind one as in a three rod wale).

NOTE: This first row of waling put on with four rods after staking-up the base is a 'pull-down wale'. Holding the basket on its side, every second stroke is pulled down firmly between the stake and bottom stick, making this first row of waling a finishing round for the edge of the base, rather than the start of the siding (Fig. 33b).

4. When the marked stake is reached leave the rod on its right (D), change-the-stroke (step-up) with the next three weavers (see Fig. 7).
5. Leave at least 7½ cm (3 in) of cane on the end of D (which you are dropping) so that it can be woven away afterwards.

UPSETTING WITH A THREE ROD WALE

1. Now sit the basket on its base and put a weight of some sort inside.
2. Continue with the three rod wale, remembering to change-the-stroke each time the mark is reached (Fig. 7). After one or two rounds, undo the string or elastic band, weave away the end D, and if the stakes stand up nicely you can leave them untied while you complete the three rows of the three rod wale.
3. As you work round the basket, pull the stakes out gently so the correct angle is obtained for an outward flow and so the basket is the right shape if it is to contain a dish. On reaching the mark, and having done one row of four rod and three rows of three rod, finish waling as in Fig. 8.
   HINT: If the stakes are still not very well 'upsett' even after the four rows of waling, put on another row or two until the stakes are standing firmly upright and the foundation of your basket is sound.
4. Cut off the ends neatly with the side cutters.

BYE-STAKES

1. Using no. 6 cane, cut twenty-eight bye-stakes, 10 cm (4 in) long.
2. Holding the basket on its side on your lap, push one bye-stake down on the right of each stake making sure they don't protrude through the base of the basket.

RANDING

This is slightly different from previous baskets as there are an even, rather than an uneven, number of stakes.

1. Start as before with a long piece of no. 3 cane. Rand in and out, in front of one stake and behind the next, until the space is reached between stakes B and C, as in Fig. 34.
2. Start another piece of no. 3 cane in the space between stakes C and D and leaving the first weaver, carry on with the second. You will see that the randing now works out correctly, in front and behind each alternate stake.
   NOTE: Because there are an even number of stakes, it is not possible to rand with a single length, as each time round the basket the weaver would go in front and behind the same stakes.
3. Carry on right round the basket with the second weaver until the first is reached again. Do *not* overtake it, stop one space to the left (between stakes A and B). Pick up the first cane and carry on randing for one round until you reach the stake to the left of the end of the second weaver (Fig. 34).
4. Continue to rand in this manner (it is sometimes called 'chasing' which aptly describes what is being done).
   PITFALL: *Never* overtake the previous row, but catch up and then go on with the second one.
5. Continue 'chasing' round with two weavers, until the band of randing is 2 cm (¾ in) deep. Make sure you have a weight inside to secure your work.
6. Bend each stake gently outwards as the weaving cane goes in front, so that the basket continues to flow outwards. Do *not* pull the cane as this will have the opposite effect as well as being very tiring on the fingers!
7. Finish the randing by leaving the ends behind a stake. Trim all the ends neatly.

Fig 34 *Chasing*

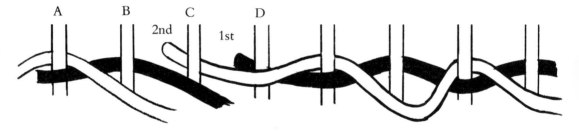

CHAIN WALING

Weave a round of chain waling as in the last basket (Figs 22–24) or do two rows of ordinary waling. If the basket is to hold a dish, place it inside to check that it fits.

RANDING

Weave another block of randing ('chasing') for a further depth of 2 cm (¾ in).

WALING

Three rounds of waling, using no. 6 cane. Remember to mark the stake to the left of the start, to change-the-stroke each time round (Fig. 7) and to finish as in Fig. 8.

Press the rows of waling down firmly as you work and check that the height of the basket is even all round. Push down to compress the weaving anywhere that is needed.

Trim off the bye-stakes.

PITFALL: Do not cut the stakes by mistake!

THREE ROD BORDER

Soak the stakes ready to bend over to weave the border, five to ten minutes in hot water, so they are really pliable (test by bending over the tip of a stake). Follow the directions as for the last basket, Figs 25–29.

FOLLOW-ON-TRAC

Finish with follow-on-trac as shown in Fig. 30. Trim all the ends neatly, making sure each end is lying against an upright stake.

5 Waste-paper basket

This basket is approx. 28 cm (11 in) high and 25½ cm (10 in) across the top. This is slightly taller than the last baskets and introduces slewing and spiral slewing. Made with a wooden base, it is more practical as small bits and pieces won't fall through the weave. I will, however, give recipes for both bases.

If you varnish or paint the base first it won't become stained with use. Children love to decorate their wooden basket bases with coloured waterproof paints. Acrylic Plastic made by Rowney and Winsor & Newton is ideal; the brushes can be washed out with water if not left for too long.

I wove this basket with a spiral weave and the directions given will be for the basket as illustrated but, of course, it could just as well be woven with randing, or another stroke of your choice. I have used dyed cane to add colour. The 'smoked' can be purchased. An easy recipe for dyeing cane is given at the end of this chapter.

MATERIAL REQUIRED

No. 8 cane (smoked) for stakes
No. 6 cane (smoked) for bye-stakes
Nos 6 and 8 cane (natural) for upsetting, waling and chain waling
No. 3 cane (natural, smoked and turquoise) for slewing – or randing if preferred
(Weight of cane approx. 200 g (7 oz))
Wooden base 18 cm (7 in) with 29 holes

METHOD WITH WOODEN BASE

Stakes

No. 8 cane (smoked) is used.

1. Cut twenty-nine stakes 60 cm (24 in). long Soak the bottom 10 cm (4 in) in hot water.
2. Check that the no. 8 cane will fit into the holes in the base; if not, insert the bodkin firmly into each hole, twisting it round to enlarge the diameter to take the no. 8 cane. NOTE: Make up a measuring stick from a piece of handle cane. Mark it clearly 60 cm (24 in). You are then much more likely to cut the stakes accurately. Keep your measuring sticks; a large coffee jar makes a good container for the different sizes you will soon collect.

FOOT BORDER

Complete this as in Chapter 1 (Figs 3 and 4). Pull all the stakes tight and bend them slightly outwards.

UPSETTING (WALING)

Work four rows of a three rod wale using no. 6 cane. Mark the stake as in Fig. 6. Change-the-stroke each time you reach the mark (as in Fig. 7). After four rounds finish carefully as in Fig. 8.

NOTE: As you work, bring the stakes into a gradual outward flow, not too much, as a waste-paper basket looks pretty awful if it comes out too far, though, of course, it would hold more waste paper!

BYE-STAKES

1. Cut two bye-stakes for each stake. Use no. 6 cane and make them 25½ cm (10 in) long.
2. Using a bodkin to widen the space, push one bye-stake in on each side of every stake, right down to the base.

SPIRAL SLEWING

Slewing is working with two or more weavers together. In order for this weave to work out properly the number of stakes must be divisible either by four minus one, or four plus one.

Fig 35 *Spiral slew*

If the wooden base is used with twenty-nine holes (4 × 7 = 28 + 1) the spiral will travel upwards to the left, clockwise.

SNAG: It is very important to have the stakes strong enough when slewing, as two or more weavers used together are twice or three times as strong as one on its own. The combined strength of the stakes and bye-stakes *must* be stronger than the weavers so your basket won't be pushed out of shape.

1. Take one length of no. 3 smoked cane and one length of no. 3 natural cane and damp them. (If you *soak* the smoked cane the colour may run.)
2. Place the smoked cane in front of two stakes

and behind two stakes, then place the natural cane beside it and work the two together. The start and end are staggered so there is no gap (Fig. 35).

3. Work round the basket (be sure to have a weight inside) taking the slew in front of two stakes and behind the next two. The natural cane should always be on top and this will help you to see that the two have not become twisted.

4. Weave slowly and carefully, bending the two stakes slightly outwards when taking the slew in front of them.

5. After you have done a few rows you will begin to see the pattern emerge (Fig. 36).

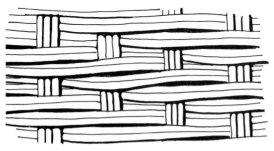

Fig 36 *Spiral slewing showing pattern*

PITFALL: If you are weaving the spiral slew correctly, each successive round will divide the pairs of the last round. So if you find that you are weaving two stakes together which were together on the last round . . . stop .   .   .
go back and find where you went wrong! Don't let me put you off, it looks really good when it is finished, it's fun to do and it grows quickly.

6. Continue to work carefully in front of two stakes and behind the next two. If you want the basket to come out a little more, ease the two stakes outwards as the slew goes in front of them. If you want the basket to continue the shape, lay the slew gently round the front of two stakes and then ease round the back of the next two stakes without distorting their position. If you feel the basket is going out too much pull the slew gently into position with each stroke until the correct shape is obtained.

NOTE: It is not usually necessary to damp the side stakes of a cane basket after it has been pricked up and upsett, until the border is reached. Weaving cane, however, should always be used damp.

Join where necessary as in randing (Fig. 10). Be careful not to join both slewing canes at the same time, and be very careful not to get the pattern wrong when joining.

7. Slew to a depth of 13 cm (5 in), pressing the cane down firmly on the row below as you work.

CHAIN WALING

Use no. 6 cane in natural. Refer to Figs 22–24 (two rows of ordinary waling can be substituted, if preferred).

SLEWING

Here three weavers in no. 3 cane are used together. For this band of decorative slewing I used two strands of smoked cane together with one strand of turquoise coloured cane for five rows.

CHAIN WALING

One more complete 'row' (twice round the basket).

SPIRAL SLEWING

Approximately three more rows, to within 2 cm (¾ in) of the top of the bye-stakes.

WALING

Weave two or three rounds of waling, using no. 8 cane (natural) to give a really firm top to the basket before the border is started.

THREE ROD BORDER

Work a three rod border as in Figs 25–29, soaking the stakes well in warm water until they are pliable so they won't crack when bent at right angles.

FOLLOW-ON-TRAC

Finish with a follow-on-trac (Fig. 30) and cut the ends off neatly inside; be very careful that all the ends are resting against a stake so they don't come through to the front and spoil the look of your basket.

METHOD WITH WOVEN BASE

No. 12 or 14 cane for bottom sticks
No. 3 cane (natural) or smoked for pairing

METHOD

1. If you wish to make the woven base, use the same pattern as in the last basket (Chapter 4) but the finished size should be 2½ cm (1 in) smaller, so cut the base sticks 19 cm (7½ in) long, and finish pairing when the base measures 15 cm (6 in) across.

2. When staking–up leave out one side stake so there are twenty-seven stakes instead of twenty-eight as in the last chapter. It is very important to have the correct number of stakes for a spiral weave.
NOTE: When planning a basket to be woven with a spiral weave the number of side stakes must be divisible by four plus one, or divisible by four minus one. In the first case the spiral twists up to the left and in the second to the right.

DYEING CANE

This is really very easy and gives exciting results!

1. Packet of Dylon hot water dye. Put together in a bucket with a tablespoon of salt.
2. Add kettle of boiling water. Wearing rubber gloves, add the cane to the mixture, swill round until it is the right colour.
3. Rinse under hot tap until the water runs clear.
NOTE: Red, black and turquoise need a lot of rinsing.

The cane can be used straight away, but wipe on a towel before weaving it into your basket. All dyed cane should be wiped after damping; a quick pull through a tissue is usually enough.

Bleached cane is good for light colours (yellow etc.). It is also less hard on the fingers and sits in place very well. It is not quite as strong as the natural unbleached cane, however.

Natural dyes

These work well. All the following were successful for natural pastel colours: laurel, elder, and pyrocanthas berries; sweet chestnut shells, onion skins, apple and yew clippings, etc.

6 Coloured needlework basket with fitted lid

It is really fun to put a bit of colour into the basket you are making, and the spiral in this basket is very easy to manage. It is woven with three colours and I used smoked, turquoise and natural. The stroke used is waling and this is woven continuously without changing-the-stroke. In order for the spiral to work out correctly the number of side stakes must be divisible by the number of weavers (in this case three) plus two, so a wooden base with twenty-nine holes is fine.

If you want to make a woven base make it with eight base sticks. Each base stick carries four side stakes which gives you thirty-two, which is also divisible by three plus two.

It is a challenge experimenting with colours and weaves, so do try it out for yourself. The recipe for dyeing cane can be found in Chapter 5.

MATERIAL REQUIRED

No. 8 cane for the side stakes (natural)
No. 6 cane for upsetting, waling, bye-stakes and the lid border (natural)
No. 3 cane for pairing and rib-randing the lid (natural and smoked)
No. 10 cane for sticks
No. 3 cane for the 'spiralled' waling (smoked, turquoise and natural)
Wooden base with 29 holes

METHOD

1. It may be necessary to enlarge the holes slightly with a bodkin to take the no. 8 cane for the stakes.
2. Follow the instructions for making the basket with a wooden base (Chapter 3) but use no. 8 cane for stakes instead of no. 6.
3. After the upset add the bye-stakes and then, instead of randing, add one length of turquoise, one of smoked and one of natural in no. 3 cane in three consecutive spaces and

start waling. You will soon see the spiral beginning to emerge.
4. Continue weaving with the three colours, joining as necessary as in Fig. 5. Complete 5 cm (2 in) of this decorative weave and finish above the starting point.

THE LEDGE

The ledge is on the inside of the basket and supports the lid. There are different ways of making a ledge but I think this is the easiest and works well.

METHOD

1. Damp five lengths of no. 8 cane, long enough to go once round the basket plus a bit to spare.
2. Mark a stake and place the five in consecutive spaces to the right of the mark. Leave about 7½ cm (3 in) ends on the inside so you can hold all five with the left hand while you weave the first few strokes to secure

Fig 37 *Starting the ledge (five rod wale)*

them. The canes can then be gently and carefully pulled in turn to 'take up the slack'.

3. Take A (Fig. 37) in front of one stake, *behind* the next four and out to the front. Do the same with B, then C, D and E. What you are doing is actually a five rod wale on the inside of the basket. As you work, you will see the long stroke on the inside which will be the ledge.

4. When the first of the five reaches the left side of the mark take A in front of one stake, behind four and out to the front. It should be lying beside the starting point of A (Fig. 38).

5. Take B in front of one, behind four and out to the front passing it under *one* cane of the previous row. It should also be lying beside a starting point.

6. Take C in front of one, behnd four and to the front under *two* canes of the previous row.

7. Take D in front of one, behind four and out under *three* canes.

8. Take E in front of one, behind four and out under *four* canes (Fig. 38).

WALING

Weave two rows using no. 6 cane (natural).

TRIM THE BYE-STAKES

Proceed as usual.

THREE ROD BORDER

This is slightly different from the previous three rod borders as it is woven from the inside of the basket instead of from the outside. When it is completed there is less of an overlap from the border to obstruct the drop-in lid.

Holding the basket in your lap, reach across to the far side and work the three rod border on the inside so that, when you bend each of the first three rods down behind the stake to its right, the ends will be brought down on the *inside* of the basket (Fig. 25).

Continue to work the three rod border as before (but from the inside). It is slightly more tricky sorting out the ends in the more confined space, but if you work slowly and carefully, following Figs 25–29, it shouldn't be too much of a problem.

Cut off the ends neatly on the inside, making sure you have finished correctly and each one is resting against another border stake and cannot pop through to the outside.

> SNAG: Do not do the follow-on-trac, as this would take up more room on the inside, defeating the object of the 'inside-out-border'.

THE LID

The construction of a lid is the same principle as a woven base, starting with a framework of strong sticks, the slath.

Fig 38 *Finishing the ledge*

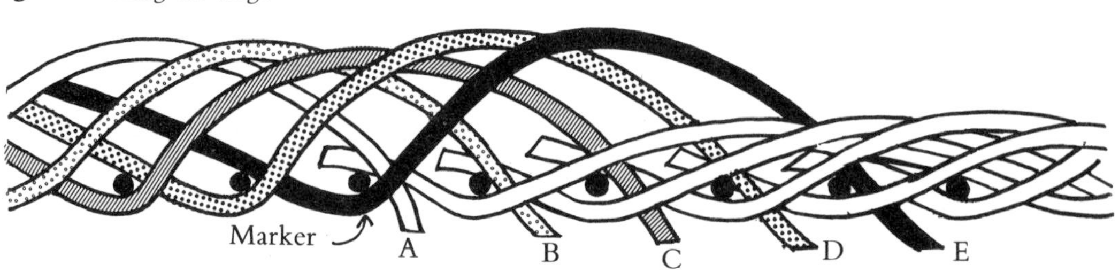

![Marker A B C D E]

42

The first thing to consider is what size it must be to fit snugly into your basket. Measure the diameter inside above the ledge. Mine measured 21 cm (8¼ in).

Now you need to know the circumference so you can work out how many stakes will be needed at the edge of the lid. It is easy enough to work out the rough circumference. You won't need a calculator.

1. Multiply the diameter by three, and add on one-seventh. In my basket the measurement was 21 cm (8¼ in).

$$21 \text{ (cm)} \times 3 = 63$$
$$21 \text{ (cm)} \div 7 = 3$$
$$\overline{66}$$

So if the circumference of the lid has to be 66 cm (26 in) to fit inside the basket, the next question is how many border stakes will be required?

2. The edge of the lid should be firm and strong so the stakes should be about 2 cm (¾–1in) apart at the border.
3. Divide 66 by 2 and the answer is 33, but there must be an even number, as each stick in the slath has two ends, so we will have thirty-two at the eedge (each approx. 2 cm (¾–1 in) apart).
4. To achieve this start with eight sticks (sixteen ends). Open out the slath, pair for 5 cm (2 in) and add another short stick to each of the sixteen ends. These are then opened out so at the border there will be thirty-two at the edge (each approx. 2 cm plete.

METHOD

1. Cut eight sticks from no. 10 cane (natural) 4 cm (1½ in) longer than the outside measurement of the top of the basket to allow ease of working. Form a slath (Fig. 13) inserting four through four. Tie in and open out, pairing with no. 3 cane, first into doubles, then singles (Fig. 21).
2. Now complete six rows of pairing with the sticks single.

RIB-RANDING

This has the same finished look as waling, but is woven with only one weaver, going in front of two sticks and behind one. It is a very suitable weave for the lid as you get a close, firm, attractive weave which hides the joining in of extra sticks. The important thing to remember when planning to rib-rand is that the number of sticks must *not* be divisible by three. As we have sixteen and then thirty-two it will work.

1. Drop one of the weavers you were pairing with and work round the lid taking the other cane in front of two sticks and behind one (Fig. 39).

Fig 39 *Rib randing*

PITFALL: Try not to miscount (better not to talk to anyone while you are doing this stroke!). If you do go wrong it is easy to unwind the cane back to the place where the error occurred.

2. Rib-rand for approximately 1 cm (½ in), joining if necessary, as in simple randing, so the joins are always on the back of the lid.

ADDING SECOND (SHORT) STICKS

Cut sixteen sticks 12 cm (4¾ in) with a slanting cut and push one down on the right side of each stick, well down into the rib-randing. These are now opened out into singles with three rounds of waling.

WALING

Mark a stick and, using no. 3 cane (I used turquoise), place three lengths of cane between three consecutive sticks to the right of the mark. Work three rounds of waling, opening out the sticks into singles. Remember to change-the-stroke each time you reach the mark and finish as in Fig. 8. By the end of these three rows the sticks and short sticks should be nicely spaced apart.

NOTE: The three cut ends of the coloured waling which will show white on the outside of the lid can be tinted with a felt pen.

The lid could be woven in pairing instead of rib-randing, but the end result is rather messy as the joining in of the additional short stakes shows through the more open weave. Every time a new length of cane is joined in the old ends are left on the outside of the lid, unlike the rib-randing where all ends are at the back.

RIB-RANDING

1. After the three rows of waling in turquoise, add four rows of rib-randing with smoked cane. This looks very effective and reflects the colours in the basket.
2. Continue rib-randing with natural cane. Shape the lid carefully so it is slightly crowned, and the sticks evenly spaced.
3. Check the inside measurement of the basket where the lid is to fit, and when the diameter of the lid is 3 cm (1¼ in) less than this measurement, finish the rib-randing by leaving the end tucked behind a stake.
   NOTE: The 3 cm (1¼ in) allows enough room for two rows of waling and the border.

WALING

Using no. 6 cane put on two rows of waling, changing-the-stroke and finishing correctly.

THREE-ROD BORDER

1. Cut thirty-two stakes from no. 6 cane, 30cm (12 in) long. Slype one end of each. Soak them well in hot water for a few minutes.
2. With the right side of the lid facing you push one stake down on the left-hand side of each stick.
3. Bend them over to the right, work a three-rod border with a follow-on-trac.
4. Trim the ends, being sure they are resting against a stake on the underside of the lid.

HANDLE

A small plait makes an effective handle. Either a three or five plait. I made a five plait with one length of natural (no. 3) bent double to make two ends, one length of turquoise treated the same way and a single length of smoked cane.

1. Thread the two ends of the natural cane through from the back of the lid (round the two middle sticks). Thread the turquoise through beside the natural, hooking its loop over the natural on the underside of the lid to hold it in place. Push the single piece of smoked through and secure it between the other two. If all else fails use some glue!
2. Plait in a similar way to a three plait. With a five plait the outside canes always come across over *two canes* instead of one as in a three plait (Fig. 40).

Fig 40 *Five plait*

3. When you have plaited 7–8 cm (3 in) push the ends through to the underside of the lid. Make sure these ends are really pliable and secure them with a reef knot tied with the natural cane, catching the turquoise and smoked within the knot. A dab of glue when the cane is dry if you are unsure of your knot.

Now stand back and admire your work – you can line the basket too if you like.

7 Hanging basket with wooden base

This is quite simple to make, and looks very attractive with almost any house plant.

Most manufactured bases have an uneven number of holes; for this basket you need an *even* number of stakes so that it balances properly. An extra stake will be added after two rows of waling. This technique can be used on any base if required.

MATERIALS REQUIRED

No. 10 cane for stakes } Natural
No. 8 cane for bye-stakes
No. 6 and 8 cane for waling
No. 3 cane for small bye-stakes } Smoked
No. 3 cane for randing
Glossy (or plain) lapping cane
Wooden base 15 cm (6 in) with 23 holes
Cork 2 cm (¾ in) diameter
Strong elastic band
Brass panel pins or tacks 1 cm (½ in)
Hammer

METHOD

1. Enlarge *every other* hole in the *wooden* base with a bodkin, so no. 10 cane will fit through. In one place two large holes will come together as there are an uneven number. Make a pencil mark on the edge of the base between these two so later you will see where to add an extra stake.
2. Cut twelve stakes from no. 10 cane 68 cm (2 ft 3 in).
3. Cut eleven stakes from no. 8 cane 46 cm (18 in).
4. In two *separate* bundles soak the ends of the no. 10 and no. 8 cane. At least ten minutes in hot water.

NOTE: The no. 10 stakes are the ones which carry the basket and are fastened to the loop at the top, the no. 8 canes (which are shorter) are turned over to form a scallop border when the basket is high enough. *They must therefore be put in alternate holes*, in one place two 10s will come together.

5. Push the damp ends of no. 10 cane through the enlarged holes in the base, so 7½ cm (3 in) protrudes on the side furthest from you.
6. Now insert the eleven stakes of no. 8 cane through the remaining alternate holes and complete the foot border as in Figs 3 and 4. Pull all the stakes tight.

UPSETTING (WALING)

No. 6 cane – smoked.

1. Start on the side *opposite* the pencil mark.
2. Weave two rounds of waling (remember to change-the-stroke), bringing the stakes out very gently.
3. Cut a piece of natural no. 8 cane 40 cm (16 in) long. Slype one end. Add it as a bye-stake

to one of the two no. 10s, either on the left of the right one or the right of the left one, so it lies between them, over the pencil mark, pushing it well down into the two rows of waling.
4. Complete two more rounds of waling, separating this 'bye-stake' from the main stake.

BYE-STAKES

Use no. 3 cane – smoked. Cut forty-eight bye-stakes 10 cm (4 in) long and push one well down on either side of each of the twenty-four stakes.

CHASING (RANDING)

Use glossy flat lapping cane and no. 3 cane – smoked.

1. Soak a length of each briefly in warm water.
2. Work a round with the lapping cane, followed by a round of the no. 3, so they chase each other, as in Fig. 34.
3. Continue until there are four rounds of each. Try to have a long enough piece of lapping cane so there is no need to join; if it is necessary, however, just overlap the lapping cane for a few strokes.

CHAIN WALING

Work one round of chain waling with no. 6 cane (natural), Figs 22–24.

CHASING

Work five more rows of chasing with glossy lapping and no. 3 cane, pulling the last row of lapping as you work to tighten the edge of the basket.

WALING

Use no. 8 cane – smoked. Work two rows, pull a little as you work to make the top of the basket really firm. Change-the-stroke and finish correctly as Figs 7 and 8.

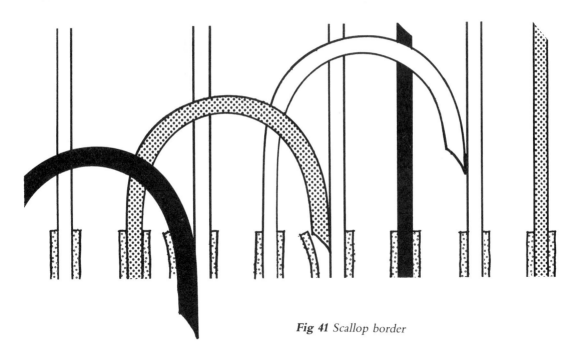

Fig 41 Scallop border

FORMING THE SCALLOP

1. Tie up the twelve no. 10 stakes so they are out of the way.
2. Trim to a point the end of one of the *short* stakes (no. 8s) and take it over to the right, in front of one no. 10 stake and down on the left-hand side of the next (in between the stake and bye-stake) and right down to the base. You may need to ease the space a little by inserting a bodkin first.
3. If this loop looks the right length, pull the stake out again, measure it, and trim the other eleven to exactly the same length and insert them round the basket (Fig. 41).

MAKING THE LOOP

Use no. 3 cane mixed smoked and natural. Work a five (or three) plait as in the handle of the needlework basket lid (Fig. 40) approx. 25 cm (10 in) long.

FINISHING OFF

1. Fit the ends of the stakes closely round a cork, secure with an elastic band, slip in the ends of the plait to form a loop of the required size. Check that none of the stakes are crossing each other and that they are equally spaced round the cork.

2. Using a bodkin, make a small hole in one of the stakes, insert a panel pin or tack and hammer home. Continue round, nailing each stake in turn to the cork. Secure the loop with two nails on each side.
3. Remove the elastic and bind a piece of Sellotape over the heads of the nails. Clip any ends of the stakes which protrude beyond the top of the cork.

BINDING

1. Damp a length of flat lapping cane.
2. Lay a short end of the cane, right side against the cork. Hold this in place with your thumb, turning the long end sharply over so the right side of the cane is now on the outside. Wrap over the end and round the cork twice.
3. Place a short piece of cane (no. 8) against the cork and wrap over this too. When the top of the cork is reached, turn the end of the lapping cane so the underside is towards you, gently remove the piece of cane and thread the end of the lapping cane through in its place.
4. Pull the end of the lapping cane, twisting the last four or five rounds to tighten them at the same time (Fig. 42).
5. Trim and secure with a small nail.

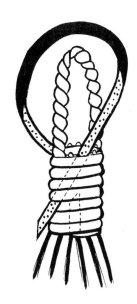

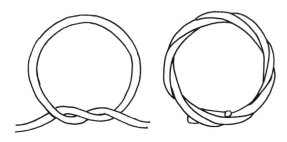

Fig 42 (left) Binding the cork

Fig 43 Simple twisted ring

SIMPLE TWISTED RINGS

Should you wish to add rings of cane to the loop on the top of the hanging basket they are quite simple to make.

Method

This method is for a loop measuring about 5 cm (2 in) across (Fig. 43).

1. A length of no. 8 cane approx. 60 cm (24 in).

2. Tie a single overhand knot in the middle of the cane and adjust to the right size.
3. Take one end and twist it two or three times round the ring and back to the knot.
4. Take the other end and twist it the opposite way round, the same number of times, placing it neatly next to the previous twists.
5. Trim the ends, one will be on either side of the ring.
6. To make an interlocking chain, the rings must be made through each other.

8 Hanging basket with woven base

This has an approx. length of 56 cm (22 in) and is slightly more difficult than the last hanging basket, but if you have managed to make the baskets with woven bases in the previous chapters, I am sure you will be able to do this without too much trouble.

MATERIALS REQUIRED

No. 10 cane for stakes
No. 8 cane for bye-stakes
No. 8 cane for waling
No. 6 cane for chain waling (smoked)
No. 3 cane for fitching (smoked)
No. 3 cane for pairing (natural)
Plain lapping cane for decorative weave and for binding the cork
Bleached cane no. 6 for Japanese twist
Cork, elastic band, panel pins or 1 cm (½ in) tacks, hammer

METHOD

1. Soak eight lengths of no. 10 cane 122 cm (48 in) and straighten any curves.
2. Make a slath as in Fig. 13, tie in and open out the stakes.
3. Shape the curve away from you, continually adjusting the stakes keeping them equally spaced and not corrugated. Press the rows of pairing firmly down on each other.
4. After about ten rows of pairing tie up the stakes with string or an elastic band. Check the symmetry of the basket, adjust so diameter is approx. 15 cm (6 in) (Fig. 44).
5. Continue pairing and shaping until you are 10 cm (4 in) from the centre of the base.

CHAIN WALING

Use no. 6 cane (smoked). Put on a band of chain

49

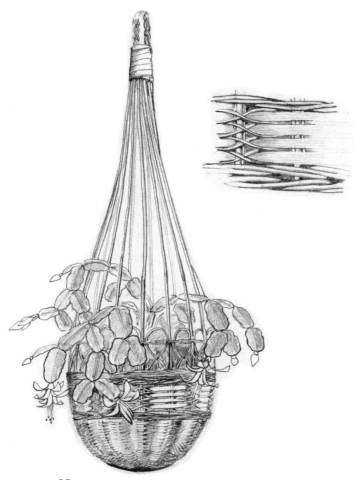

Fig 44 (below left) Stakes tied

waling, mark the start, change-the-stroke and
finish as in Figs 22–24.

JAPANESE TWIST

This decorative weave was illustrated in a
Japanese book; as I couldn't understand the
script I have given it a name which may not be
the correct one.

1. Soak a piece of flat lapping cane, place the
   short end behind one stake, in front of one
   and behind the next two, and out to the
   front.

   NOTE: When randing with flat lapping cane,
   start by taking the cane behind one stake,
   in front of one and behind the next two
   before starting to rand in and out. This pre-
   vents the gap caused by the second row

10 cm

15 cm

50

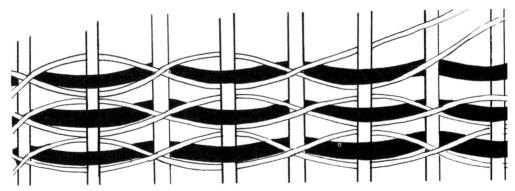

Fig 45 *Japanese twist*

climbing on top of the first. Finish by going behind two and in front of one over the starting place.

2. Now with two pieces of bleached cane (no. 6) insert one above and one below the lapping cane (Fig. 45).

   NOTE: Bleached cane is much softer and more pliable (almost like spaghetti!) so is very suitable for this weave, it sits well in place. For general work it is not usually as strong as the natural cane, but it is much less hard on the fingers and so may be easier for some to manage.

3. Cross the two bleached canes (as in pairing) in front of the same stake, and, taking one on either side of the lapping cane, weave them behind the next stake and out to the front again on either side of the lapping cane.

4. Now the lapping cane is taken in front of the stake to its right, behind the next and out to the front.

5. The two no. 6s are now crossed again and continued as before, in and out of the same stakes, round the basket until four rows have been completed.

CHAIN WALING

One round of chain waling using no. 6 cane (smoked).

WALING

Finish with two rows of waling using no. 8 cane (natural) pulling slightly as you work to keep the top nice and firm.

FITCHING

Use no. 3 cane (smoked). This is working with a pair of weavers, twisting them in a similar way to reverse pairing, either once or twice between each stake. It is used to bind the stakes firmly together after a space has been created in a basket.

1. Keep the stakes tied at the top, take a length of cane, soak it in warm water and bend it round one of the stakes approx. 4 cm (1½ in) from the top of the wale, bringing the two ends out towards you.

2. Twist the canes over with your right hand as though you are turning a key anticlockwise. The cane furthest from you (the one which came from behind the first stake) comes over the top of the second which is then taken behind the next stake to the right and out to the front (Fig. 46).

3. Continue round, keeping the fitch the same height above the wale until you have completed one round.

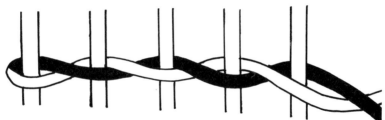

Fig 46 *Fitching*

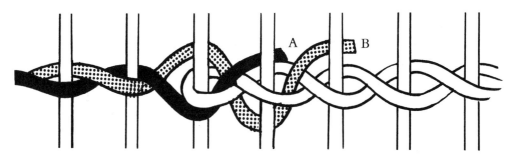

Fig 47 *Finishing fitching*

4. Finish off, threading A up through the starting loop and resting it behind the next stake

5. Take B down through the loop, behind the next stake and up through the next loop. SNAG: Do not cut the ends off too short until the next stage, adding bye-stakes, is complete.

BYE-STAKES

Use no. 8 cane (natural).

1. Cut sixteen bye-stakes 25 cm (10 in) long with a slanting cut.

2. Insert one end through the fitching on the right side of stake A, cross over and push the end down beside the left side of B, well down through the decorative weave, approx. 5 cm (2 in).

3. Bring the other end through the fitching on the left side of stake B. Cross in front and ease the end well down into the weave so a loop is formed about 5 cm (2 in) above the waling (Fig. 48). SNAG: The bye-stakes should remain damp throughout, otherwise they may kink instead of bending smoothly.

4. Adjust the loops as you work so they are all approximately the same height.

5. Remove the string which is tying the stakes. Snip off any ends which are protruding inside the basket, being careful not to cut them too short.

FINISHING OFF

Exactly as in the last basket.

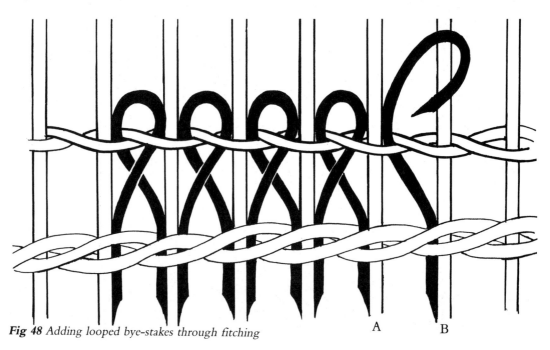

Fig 48 *Adding looped bye-stakes through fitching*

A   B

9 Oval tray with a wooden base

The one illustrated measured 30 × 20 cm (12 × 8 in). This chapter gives instruction on how to make a tray with a *simple* but very effective 'plait' border. I used a wooden base stained with light mahogany and varnished.

MATERIAL REQUIRED

No. 6 cane for stakes (natural)
No. 6 cane for bye-stakes (smoked or natural)
No. 3 cane for waling
Wooden or melamine tray base
Coloured wooden beads, if required for handles
  (I used green)

METHOD

1. Cut one stake for each hole, no. 6 cane, 25 cm (10 in).
2. Soak the ends and work foot border as in Figs 3 and 4.

THE UPSETT

Either work five rows of waling with no. 3 cane, remembering to change-the-stroke (Fig. 7) and finish (Fig. 8). Or, if beads are required to add colour and form a 'handle', add them after three rows of waling, threading them on to the stakes at each end. Weave one row of pairing right round the tray and over the beads, finishing with another two rows of waling. The row of pairing helps to prevent the beads being pushed out of place by the waling.

SNAG: Be careful not to pull the weavers as you work the waling; a tray looks much better if the side comes straight up rather than being pulled inwards.

BYE-STAKES

Cut 15 cm (6 in) bye-stakes, one for each hole in the base, in either natural or smoked, and push firmly through the waling to the base on the right of each stake.

NOTE: The beads are threaded on to the main stake, the bye-stake lies beside.

SIMPLE JAPANESE PLAIT BORDER

1. Damp the stakes so they are pliable.
   PITFALL: Be careful if you are using coloured cane with the natural not to over-wet the stakes so the colour runs.
2. Working round the border bend each pair down behind the pair to their right and out to the front so all are pointing out sideways and the two are lying flat beside each other firmly on top of the waling (Fig. 49).
3. To finish the first stage, tuck the last pair through the first which were bent over.
4. *Second stage*
   Take all the ends to the inside exactly like a follow-on-trac (Fig. 50).
5. *Third stage*
   The ends can *either* be cut off inside (being *very* careful to see they are lying behind a stake) *or* a further trac can be woven to give a thicker and firmer border. (At this stage the ends should not be longer than 7–8 cm (3 in) otherwise it is rather muddling; so trim them if they are too long.)

(a) Working from left to right, take each pair in turn, in front of one pair to its right and leave it tucked behind the next (Fig. 51). Continue round the inside until the last pair. This is tucked in under the pair at the start.

(b) All the ends can now be cut off neatly inside.

PITFALL: Do not cut the ends too short or they may come undone later on.

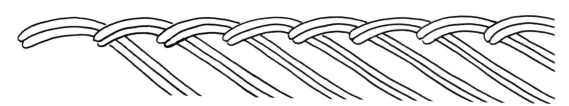

Fig 49 *Starting simple Japanese plait*

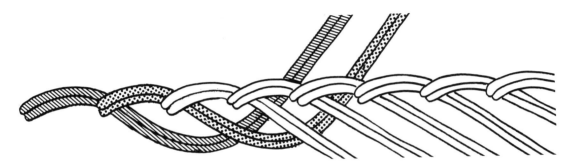

Fig 50 *Continuing simple Japanese plait*

Fig 51 *Finishing simple Japanese plait*

10 Oval tray with a woven base

The base measures 36 × 23 cm (14 × 9 in). Oval bases are slightly more complicated than round ones but if you understand a few basic rules, *and have worked your way through this book!* you won't find it too difficult to make this small oval tray.

The base for an oval basket consists of a slath made from three, four or five long sticks threaded through a number of shorter ones. The number used is decided by the required circumference of the basket, how many stakes will be required at the border (so they are not too far apart) and how many bottom sticks will be needed to 'carry' those side stakes.

Unlike a round basket, not every stick in an oval base will carry two side stakes beside each of its ends (Fig. 52).

People are often worried by the fact that the oval base is inclined to twist when it is woven with pairing. This problem of a twisting oval base need not occur if it is woven with randing, either chasing and/or rib-randing as I have done

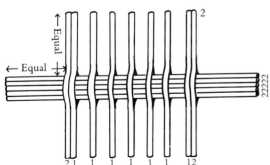

Fig 52 *Oval slath showing number of stakes to each stick*

in this oval tray. It is also very important to have the strongest possible cane for the base sticks.

MATERIAL REQUIRED

For the base
  No. 15 cane for base sticks (natural)
  No. 3 chair seating cane to wrap the slath
  No. 8 cane (two short pieces) (natural)
  No. 3 cane for randing and rib-randing (natural, smoked and coloured)

No. 6 cane for waling (natural)

For the side of the tray
  No. 8 cane for side stakes (natural)
  No. 3 cane for the upsett (smoked)
  String
  (Weight of cane approx. 150 g (6 oz))

METHOD

1. Cut five base sticks 40½ cm (16 in) and nine sticks 27 cm (10½ in).
2. Soak in hot water for five minutes.
3. Pierce the short sticks and thread the long ones through.
4. Wrap eight times round with the chair cane between each bottom stick (diagram shows only four or five) after arranging them as shown (Fig. 53). This will hold them in place and each will be equally spaced 2 cm (¾ in) apart.
5. Slide a short piece of no. 8 cane in through the slit in the short sticks on either side of the wrapped slath. This stops the weaving from becoming 'waisted' at the sides (Fig. 54).

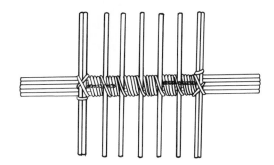

Fig 53 *Oval slath (underside) bound with chair cane*

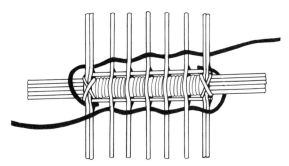

Fig 54 *Bound slath, showing added length of no. 8 cane and start of randing (chasing)*

6. Take two lengths of damp no. 3 cane and insert 1 cm (½ in) of each at opposite ends of the slath.

   NOTE: These two will be chasing each other, each going in front and behind alternate sticks. Therefore one starts by going in front of the group of long sticks at one end, and the other by going behind the group of long sticks at the other end (Fig. 54).

7. Tie in the slath with two bands of randing round the groups of sticks.

8. Open out the sticks into singles, and rand round firmly, spacing them evenly (Fig. 55).

   NOTE: You will need to use the tip of a bodkin to help you push the rows of randing firmly down between the sticks you are opening out.

9. After six or eight rows (2 cm (¾ in)) the sticks should be evenly spaced.

RIB-RANDING

Use no. 3 cane, with one cane but going behind one stick and in front of two each time (Fig. 39). The number of sticks must not be divisible by three.

NOTE: Aim to keep the base flat all the time while you work as it is for a tray. If it was to be staked up for a basket you would 'crown' the base.

1. Drop one weaver and rib-rand (Fig. 39) with natural cane for 1 cm (½ in).

2. Change to smoked cane and rib-rand for 1 cm (½ in) or else weave a round of chain waling.

3. Change to coloured cane (I used red) and rib-rand for 2½ cm (1 in).

4. Change to natural and rib-rand for 2 cm (¾ in).

5. Change to smoked and rib-rand for another 1 cm (½ in) or chain wale.

   NOTE: The tray could, of course, be woven entirely with natural cane if you prefer. In this case just continue rib-randing until the base measures approx. 35 × 22 cm (13¾ × 8 in) across and then follow step 6, leaving out 2–5.

6. Finally change to no. 6 cane (natural) and wale for three rows. Use long lengths this time so they go at least once round the base without running out.

   Keep the base flat as you work and at the same time pull the cane gently with each stroke to keep the edge of the base firm. Work three rows, remembering to change-the-stroke and finish correctly (Figs 7 and 8).

STAKING-UP

1. Cut forty-two side stakes from no. 8 cane (natural) 35 cm (14 in), point one end of each and soak them in hot water for about 5 minutes.

2. Insert them at least 7½ cm (3 in), two beside each of the end sticks and one beside each of the side sticks, as numbered in Figs 52 and 55.

Fig 55 *Opened-out oval slath*

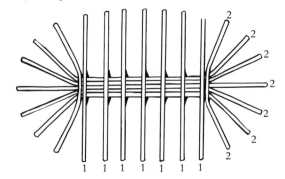

3. Squeeze each with round-nosed pliers so they will bend. Tie up the stakes in three lots (ten in the middle and sixteen at each end).

THE UPSETT

This uses no. 3 cane (smoked). One row of four rod pull-down wale, five rows three rod wale.

1. Work a four rod pull-down wale as in Figs 33 a and b. After each stroke give the cane a pull to keep it tight and bend the base slightly concave at the same time. Join as necessary (Fig. 5) but not too near the change-of-stroke and preferably not in the first row of the four rod wale.
2. Change-the-stroke (D, C, B, A) when you reach the start and leave one of the four rods (which ever is the shortest) cutting it to an end long enough to tuck away later.
3. Stand the base on a table with a weight inside and work a three rod wale (Figs 6–8), pulling the canes firmly enough to keep the waling tight and the stakes going straight upwards.
4. After three rows undo the string and if the stakes are well 'set up' continue without it, waling firmly, shaping the edge of the tray and adjusting the stakes as necessary.
5. Continue for five rows, changing-the-stroke each row and finishing off correctly as in Fig. 8.

PLAIT BORDER

You can either work the small simple plait as in the last tray, or try the traditional three-pair plait that follows. I think you will find it easiest to make a good plait if you stand directly over the border as you work.

NOTE: Make sure you have a weight inside the tray to anchor it firmly.
1. Damp the stakes, being careful not to get the whole tray too wet or the colours *may* run.
2. Cut two pieces of no. 8 cane 10 cm (4 in) and three pieces the length of the stake above the wale plus about 5 cm (2 in).
   NOTE: It is *very* important to have these pieces the same size as the border stakes.
3. Squeeze all the stakes ½ cm (¼ in) above the top of the wale with round nosed pliers.

4. Place one of the short canes between two stakes, but not directly over the finish of the waling. Bend the stake on its left down over it and place one of the long pieces beside it *leaving at least 5 cm (2 in) on the inside of the tray for finishing at the end* (Fig. 56a).

Fig 56a Starting three pair plait

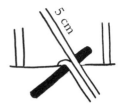

5. Put in the second short piece, making sure it overlaps the first two strands on the outside, and place the second long piece beside it leaving 5 cm (2 in) inside as before (Fig. 56b).

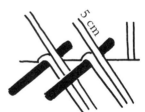

Fig 56b

6. Pick up the first two on the left and bring them through to the inside between the next two standing stakes, bend down the left of these two and place the last long piece beside it (Fig. 56c).

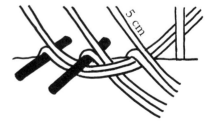

Fig 56c

Now all the extra pieces of cane are in place; each should have a 5 cm (2 in) end pointing to the left on the inside of the tray. There is now one pair on the inside and two pairs on the outside (Fig. 56c).

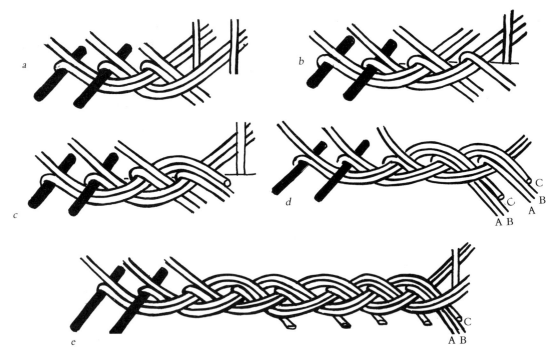

Fig 57 *Continuing three pair plait*

7. Pick up the left-hand pair on the outside ('Pick up two') and take them between the next two stakes to the right ('Take them through') (Fig. 57a).

   Bend down the left stake ('Bend down the stake') (Fig. 57b) and bring out the left-hand pair beside it ('And bring out two') making the first group of three on the outside (Fig. 57c).

8. Repeat this movement, picking up the left-hand pair on the outside:

   'Pick up two,
   Take them through,
   Bend down the stake,
   And bring out two.'

   There should now be three stakes in each of the two groups on the outside and one pair on the inside (Fig. 57d).

   NOTE: Each time you 'Pick up two' it means A and B; C is left behind and trimmed off at the end. *It is most important* to take the correct two, A and B, *NOT* C (Fig. 57e). The plait must be kept in place with one hand while the other is free to complete the next stroke.

9. The plait continues with three distinct movements:

(a) 'Pick up two', lifting with the back of the left thumb while holding the other four stakes below.

(b) 'Take them through' with the right hand which then holds them in place.

(c) 'Bend down the stake' with the left thumb, easing it over firmly on top of the border. Everything is now held secure by this stroke, leaving the right hand free to

(d) 'Bring out two'.

Continue round the border until you have been right round and there are no stakes left standing upright (Fig. 58a).

TO FINISH

1. Pick up two (A and B) and take them through over the last three brought out and under the first bent-over stake in place of the first short stick which can now be removed (Fig. 58b).

2. Pick up two again, the last A and B on the outside and take them through, following *exactly* where the second short stick lies *over* the first pair. Now remove the short stick, the work will resemble Fig. 59a.

3. There are now three single ends pointing

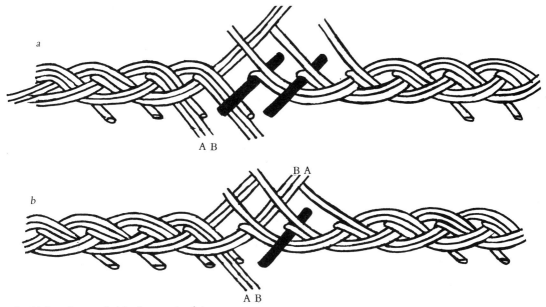

Fig 58 Starting to finish three pair plait

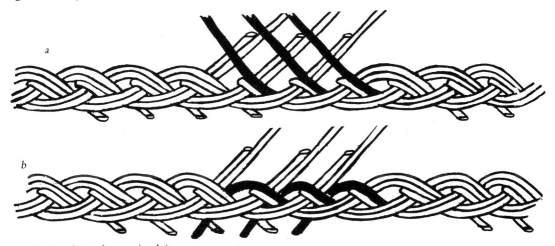

Fig 59 Finishing three pair plait

left and three pairs (shaded) pointing right. Weave the single long ends away under the border and out to the front (Fig. 59b). Weave the right-hand one of each pair (shaded) into the border following the pattern (Fig. 60). Cut off the three remaining ends on the inside. Turn the tray upside down and trim the ends closely to the underside of the plait (Fig. 60).

Fig 60 Finished plait

11 Child's shopping basket

This 25½ cm (10 in) long, 9 cm (3½ in) high basket is a simplified version of the traditional square-based basket and can easily be managed by anyone who has worked their way success-fully through this book.

Instead of the base being made first and then the side stakes being driven into it with the help of a bodkin (sometimes a difficult and tedious job), the stakes are woven into the base as the work progresses. These stakes are known as leagues or runners and consist of a single length worked through the bottom into both sides and ends and into the border.

You will need a screw-block to hold the base sticks in place as you work. You could make one of the dimensions given. It is larger than necessary for this little basket, but when you go on to bigger baskets and perhaps willow

work, you will find it invaluable. It is better to have the screw-block a little larger, than too small and light. A heavier one stays firmly in place while you work and makes the whole job much easier.

SCREW BLOCK

Two pieces of wood 5 × 5 × 80 cm (2 × 2 × 32 in).
Two coach bolts 14 cm (5½ in) long and approx. 10 mm (⅜ in) diameter.
Two wing nuts and washers to fit the bolts.

The wood should have two holes drilled 15 cm (6 in) in from each end. The holes should fit the bolts but they must be loose enough so the two pieces of wood can be screwed tightly together (Fig. 2)

MATERIAL REQUIRED

No. 15 cane for base sticks, corner posts and handle bows
No. 8 cane (smoked or dyed for side stakes)
No. 3 cane (preferably bleached) for weaving the base
No. 6 cane (natural) for upsetting and waling
Glossy lapping cane for randing and wrapping handles
No. 3 cane (dyed – I used turquoise) for slewing and handle decoration
(Weight 150 g (6 oz))

METHOD

1. Cut seven sticks 35 cm (14 in) from no. 15 cane, soak and straighten them if necessary. Place in the screw-block as shown in Fig. 61, two together at each edge and the others spaced 3 cm (1¼ in) apart.
   NOTE: There *must* be an uneven number of base sticks for this design.
2. Cut five stakes from no. 8 cane 1 m (40 in). *Try to use smoked or dyed cane; it is much easier to work this base and to see where the stakes are if they are a different colour from the base randing.*
3. Damp the stakes and squeeze each one 38 cm (15 in) from one end with the round nosed pliers so it will bend at a right angle.
4. Tie the long end to stick number 2 with two ties so that the right angle rests on the screw-

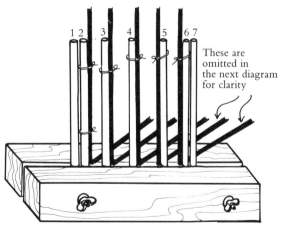

These are omitted in the next diagram for clarity

Fig 61 *Sticks in screw-block with first stakes tied*

block with the 38 cm (15 in) end pointing away from you. (Twist ties from freezer bags are ideal for this.)

5. Place one of these stakes beside each of the three single base sticks and one on the inside beside each pair, tying each one to its base stick with one or two ties.
   NOTE: The inside one of the 'pairs' *only* is tied to the stake (Fig. 61).

PAIRING

Take a length of dampened no. 3 bleached cane (or natural which has been soaked for at least five minutes in hot water). Bend it round the left-hand pair of sticks (1 and 2) and the stake so that there is approximately 20 cm (8 in) of cane on the left and the rest lies to the front between sticks 2 and 3. Starting on the left, pair across the bottom sticks and stakes once (as in Fig. 62) to the right-hand edge. The long end is left resting against the back and the short end against the front.

Fig 62 *Insertion of 'league' (side stake)*

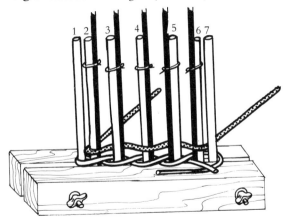

ADDING FIRST SIDE STAKE (OR LEAGUE)

1. Now cut eight more stakes from no. 8 cane (same colour as the other stakes tied to the base sticks) 90 cm (3 ft) long.
2. Damp them and find the middle of one which is hooked over stick 4. One side is woven behind 3 and the other behind 5 (Fig. 62).
3. Squeeze this stake with the round nosed pliers at each side where it is to be bent at a right angle and taken between the two pairs of end sticks, 1 and 2, 6 and 7, to form the first pair of side stakes. You may need to push the stakes down between the sticks with the tip of a bodkin to get them firmly in place.

RANDING

1. Pick up the cane lying at the back of the right-hand pair of sticks, and follow Fig.

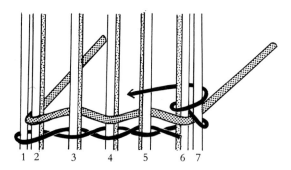

Fig 63 Showing direction of randing following insertion of first stake

63. Bring the cane round 7 to the front, between 6 and 7 to the back, encircle 6 and 7 (anti-clockwise) and rand across to the left-hand edge, in and out of the opposite sticks to those of the new stake you have just inserted.
2. At the left edge, follow Fig. 64. Bring the cane behind 2 and to the front between 1 and 2, now between 2 and 3 to the back and encircle 1 and 2 (anti-clockwise). Rand back across to the right side of the base.
   NOTE: It is important to put in the correct sequence at both ends after inserting each stake, otherwise the two sticks at each edge

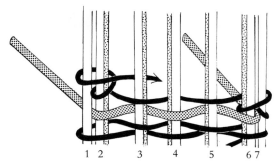

Fig 64 Continuation of randing following insertion of first stake

would not be tied together tightly and the randing would not work out in front and behind the correct sticks.

3. Rand backwards and forwards across the base; every second row make a complete turn round the pair of sticks at each end, to keep the randing level and the sides covered by the cane. Join as necessary (Fig. 10) old and new ends on the side nearest you and preferably resting against the middle stick.
   SNAG: It is terribly important to keep the cane that you are randing really damp as it looks awful if it cracks or splits when taken round the outside sticks. Bleached cane is much less likely to crack.
4. Rand for a depth of not more than 3 cm (1¼ in) and then put in one of the seven remaining side stakes.
   NOTE: Each new stake is inserted in exactly the same way as the first one illustrated in Fig. 62.
   PITFALL: Be very careful not to have the randing between the stakes any deeper than 3 cm (1¼ in) as this would mean that the stakes would be too far apart at the edge and so the border would be flimsy.
5. Because there are an uneven number of sticks, this time the end of the randing cane will be lying below the newly inserted stake on the *left*-hand side of the base. Follow Fig. 65. Take the randing cane from the back, round the edge to the front, between 1 and 2 and now round 2 to the front, encircle 2 and 1 (clockwise) and rand back across to the right side of the base. Now follow Fig. 66. Round behind 6, between 6 and 7 to the front, round 6 to the back and encircle 7 and 6 (clockwise) and rand back across the base.
   NOTE: Continue randing the base back-

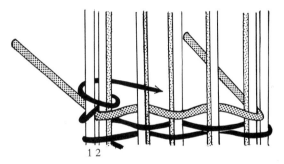

Fig 65 *Showing direction of randing following insertion of second stake*

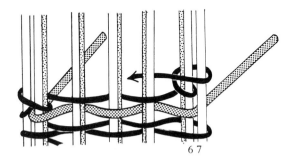

Fig 66 *Continuation of randing following insertion of second stake*

wards and forwards, wrapping twice round the edge every second row, and inserting another league (side stake) every 3 cm (1¼ in). Follow the diagrams in order, 63 and then 64 on each side of the first stake inserted, 65 and then 66 on each side of the next. So, every odd-numbered stake, Figs 63 and 64 will apply. Every even-numbered stake, Figs 65 and 66 will apply (so long as the *first* row of pairing ends on the right). PITFALL: Measure the width of your work constantly. Make yourself a stick exactly the width of the woven base at the screw-block. Check every few rows that the base is not being pulled inwards; this is a common tendency.

6. When the last of the eight side stakes has been inserted, rand once more across the base and bring the end round to the front. Start back across the base, behind the next stick and then under the previous row of randing and out to the front again. Repeat this, in front of one, behind one and under the previous row, leaving the end against the pair of end sticks. This puts a final row

of 'pairing' on the base and keeps all the weaving secure while the upsett is woven (Fig. 67).

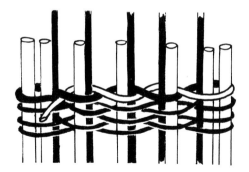

Fig 67 *'Paired' top of finished base*

Remove the base from the screw-block and *very carefully* cut off the protruding ends of the base sticks. Whatever you do, don't cut the side stakes instead!

Tie up the stakes with string or an elastic band.

THE UPSETT

This basket takes four rows of three rod waling.

1. Starting at one end weave one row of a three rod wale and then undo the two stakes at each of the four corners to stop them being pulled inwards.

2. After the second row has been completed (don't forget to change-the-stroke), cut four short pieces of no. 15 cane 10 cm (4 in). Slype one end and push one down into the waling at each corner between the two corner stakes. They must go right through to the base where they will be cut off flush, fitting neatly between the two end sticks. NOTE: These corner posts must be cut from thick cane if they are to do their job properly – keeping the corners of the basket nice and square.

3. Finish the four rows of upsetting correctly (Fig. 8).

BYE-STAKES

Cut one bye-stake for each stake 7½ cm (3 in) in the same colour as the stakes, and insert on right of each stake.

RANDING (CHASING)

Eight rows, using glossy lapping cane alternately slewing with two coloured no. 3s (Fig. 34). (I used turquoise and it looked lovely. The smoked stakes made a dark border, contrasting with the rest of the basket which was in natural cane.)

Carefully adjust the stakes as you work, particularly at the corners to prevent them from being pulled inwards.

WALING

Three rows in natural cane no. 6.

THREE ROD BORDER WITH FOLLOW-ON-TRAC *(Figs 25–30)*

Damp the stakes well but avoid getting the rest of the basket wet, especially if you have used dyed cane. Keep the corners as square as you can. It is possible to reverse the sequence of bordering the stakes at the corners to make them really square, but it is rather advanced and not really necessary on a small basket without a lid.

Finish with the follow-on-trac and cut the ends off neatly inside, being sure they are resting against a stake so they will not pop through to the outside.

HANDLE

1. Cut two pieces of no. 15 cane (which have been soaked for five minutes) 51 cm (20 in) and slype the ends.
   NOTE: These two pieces must be *exactly* the same size.
2. Insert them (right down through the weaving to the base) on the left side of the left middle stake and the right of the right middle stake.
3. Wrap a piece of Sellotape across the two to hold them together at the top.
4. Take a piece of glossy lapping cane about 2 m (6ft 6 in). Soak it and slype one end, and push this short end up through the waling on the left of one of the handles. Take the long end diagonally across the front from left to right, over the border, down the inside behind the waling, out under the waling still on the right, and diagonally across top left (Fig. 68).

Fig 68 *Start of wrapping the handle*

5. Now start to wrap round the handle bow taking in the short end. After about seventeen or eighteen wraps include the second handle bow and wrap the two together for about sixteen wraps, and then continue down one handle bow on the opposite side of the basket to the border, finishing with a cross on the outside of the waling as at the start, and taking the end away securely behind the last row of randing.

Fig 69 *Continuing to wrap the handle*

6. Take another 2 m (6ft 6 in) length of lapping cane and follow the same directions with the unwrapped handle bow, wrapping over the two again. This time a piece of coloured lapping cane can be added to continue the colour in the slewing, wrapping under and over it (Fig. 69). Join if necessary (Fig. 70). SNAG: The wrapping takes more cane than you might expect.

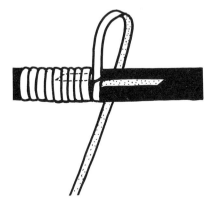

Fig 70 *Join for handle wrapping*

PEGGING THE HANDLE

Handle bows must always be pegged to stop them coming loose. This is done by driving a bodkin obliquely through the waling and the bow from outside to inside and then tapping a piece of slyped no. 6 cane through with a hammer when the bodkin is removed. The ends are cut off neatly and the handle will be secure. Glue the pegs if you like (Fig. 69).

Finishing the basket

SINGEING

This can be done to remove the 'hairs'. First damp the basket so that it isn't scorched and, using a methylated spirit flame or a butane gas blowtorch, pass the basket across the flame to and fro until all the hairs are singed off.

VARNISH

Sometimes it helps to firm up a basket to give it a coat of matt polyurethane and it also helps to bring out the different colours. Coloured polyurethane, such as oak or dark oak, gives the cane the look of fine willow. Shellac wood sealer seals the surface of the cane, helping it to resist dirt. However, some people never varnish their baskets and say that washing frequently in warm water is the best way to keep them clean and dust free.

Cane sizes

This table shows sizes of cane to use if you now wish to design your own basket.

Type of basket	Cane size no.	Maximum distance apart at border	
		cm	in
Child's small			
Base sticks	8–10		
Side stakes	6–8	2–2½	¾–1
Weavers	3–5		
Shopping (medium size)			
Base sticks	10–12		
Side stakes	8–10	2–3	¾–1¼
Weavers	5–6		
Shopping (large size)			
Base sticks	12–15		
Side stakes	10–12	2½–4½	1–1¾
Weavers	6–8		
Linen basket			
Base sticks	15		
Side stakes	12	3–4½	1¼–1¾
Weavers	6–8		
Log basket			
Base sticks	Handle cane (8 mm)		
Side stakes	15	4–6	1½–2¼
Weavers	6–8		
Miniature work			
Stakes and sticks	1–3	1–1½	⅜– ⅝
Weavers	000–0		

Length of stakes required above waling for borders illustrated in this book

	cm	in	
Scallop border (mat)	13	5	
Trac border (small mats)	18	7	
Trac border (large mats)	20	8	**Note:** Conversion from metric to imperial measurements is approximate.
Three rod	20	8	
Follow-on-trac	13	5	
Japanese plait	20	8	
Three pair plait	26	10	

Bibliography

Butcher, Mary, *Willow Work*, Dryad Press.

Crampton, Charles, *Canework*, 24th Edition, Dryad Press.

Crampton, Charles, *The Junior Basket Maker*, Dryad Press.

Dunwell, Jack, *Centre Cane Baskets, Hazards and Hints*, Hadden Best & Co. (Supplied by J. Dunwell, 41 Jackson Road, East Barnet, London EN4 8UT)

Elton Barratt, Olivia, *Rushwork*, Dryad Press.

Maynard, Barbara, *Modern Basketry from the Start*, G. Bell & Sons.

Maynard, Barbara, *Basketry (in easy steps)*, Studio Vista.

Maynard, Barbara and Deutch, *Basketry for Everyone*, Cavendish House.

Wright, Dorothy, *Baskets and Basketry*, David & Charles.

Wright, Dorothy, *A Caneworker's Book for the Senior Basket Maker*, Dryad Press.

Suppliers

Dryad
PO Box 38
Northgates
Leicester LE1 9BU
Tel. 0533 50405

Reeves Dryad
178 Kensington High Street
London
Tel. 01 937 5370

Dunlicraft
Pullman Road
Wigston
Leicester LE1 6DY
Tel. 0533 811040

Frank Herring
27 Higher West Street
Dorchester
Dorset
Tel. 0305 67917

Jacob Young & Westbury
JYW House
Bridge Road
Haywards Heath
Sussex RH16 1TZ
Tel. 0444 412411

Smit & Co. Ltd
99 Walnut Tree Close
Guildford
Surrey GU1 4UQ
Tel. 0483 33113

The Cane Store
377 Seven Sisters Road
London N15
Tel. 01-802 8195

L.H. Turtles Ltd
10 Park Street
Croydon
Surrey
Tel. 01-648 5513

THE BASKETMAKERS' ASSOCIATION

The Basketmakers' Association was formed to help promote the knowledge of basketry and allied crafts, through the provision of courses and workshops. It also helps to assure the continuing supply of materials and tools necessary for the craft.

Membership is open to all who are interested and application forms may be obtained from Olivia Elton Barratt, Millfield Cottage, Little Hadham, Ware, Herts SG11 2ED.

Index